Number 13

Hot Rodding
INTERNATIONAL

Contents

Front cover photo: From Pat Ganahl's regular online blogs comes this photo taken by the late Fred Enke in 1967. Pat's "Pickin's" blog is featured this issue, starting on page 86.

Published in 2021 by Graffiti Publications Pty. Ltd.
69 Forest Street, Castlemaine, 3450, Victoria, Australia
Phone International: 61 3 5472 3653 or 61 3 5472 3805.
Email: info@graffitipub.com.au
Website; www.graffitipub.com.au
Publisher/Editor: Larry O'Toole
Text & Production: Larry O'Toole, Al O'Toole, Mary-Anna Brennand
Sales & Marketing: Mary O'Toole, Wendy Thomas
Photos: Larry O'Toole, Al O'Toole, Mary O'Toole, Greg Stokes, Craig Stare, Darron Davies, Lara O'Toole.

The information in this publication is true and complete to the best of our knowledge. All recommendations are made without any guarantee on the part of the author or publisher, who also disclaim any liability incurred in connection with the use of this data or specific details.

We recognise that some words, model names and designations mentioned herein, are the property of the trademark holder. We use them for identification purposes only. This is not an official publication.

Graffiti Publications titles are also available at discounts in bulk quantity for industrial or sales promotional use. For details contact Graffiti Publications Ph: (613) 5472 3653.
Printed & bound in Singapore by SC (Sang Choy) International Pte Ltd.
ISSN: 1836-2850. ISBN: 978-0-949398-69-7

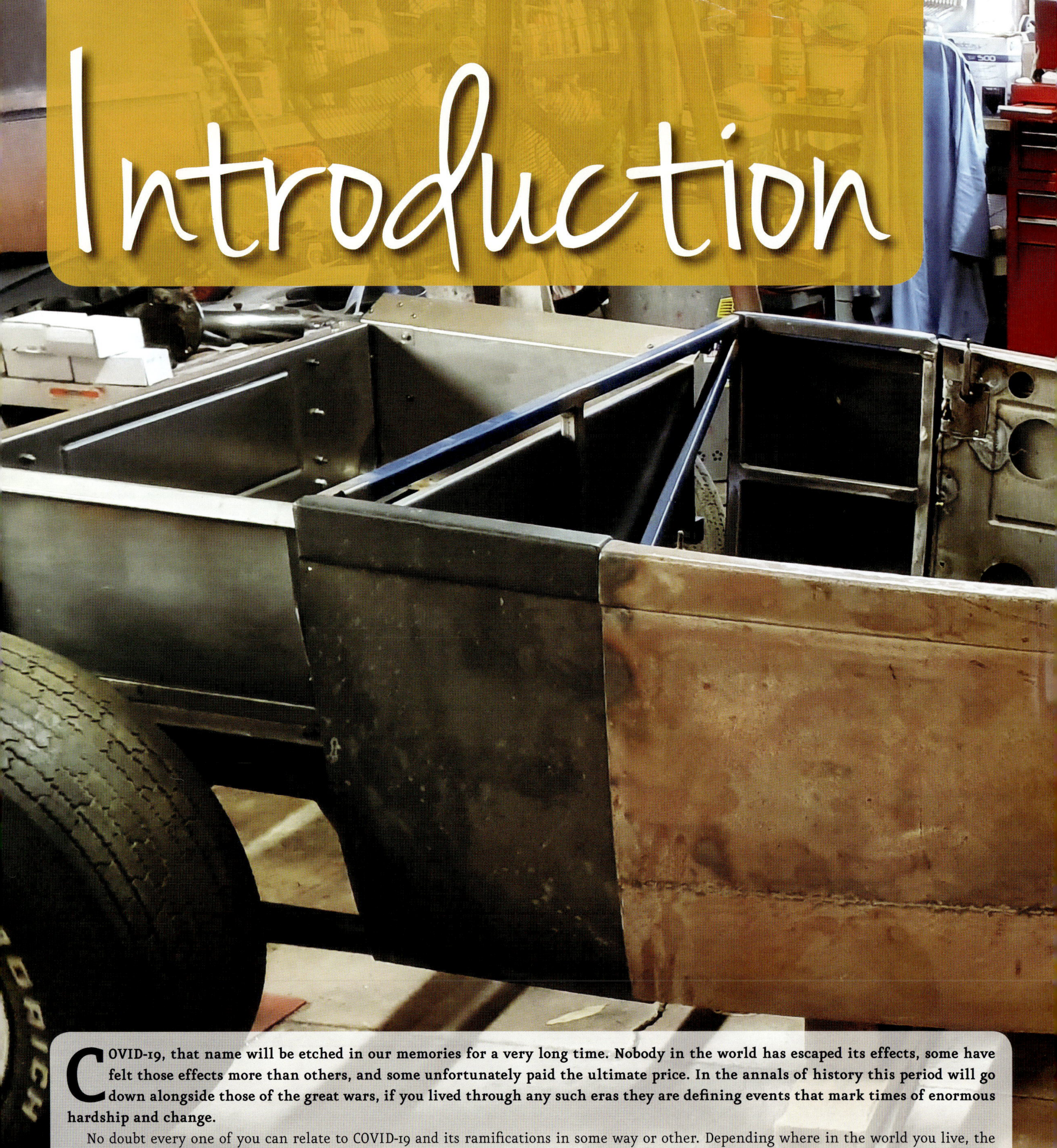

Introduction

COVID-19, that name will be etched in our memories for a very long time. Nobody in the world has escaped its effects, some have felt those effects more than others, and some unfortunately paid the ultimate price. In the annals of history this period will go down alongside those of the great wars, if you lived through any such eras they are defining events that mark times of enormous hardship and change.

No doubt every one of you can relate to COVID-19 and its ramifications in some way or other. Depending where in the world you live, the repercussions have been different. In Europe and North America the adverse effects of COVID-19 have certainly been more severe than they have for us in our part of the southern hemisphere, more particularly in Australia and New Zealand. While we did have to deal with outbreaks of COVID in Australia, it was never anywhere near as disastrous as it was elsewhere, mostly due to fast reactions by our governments that were seen as overly severe by most of our populace at the time, but in retrospect it was this action that saw us deal with it and ultimately contain it much better than almost anywhere else in the world.

Narrow our focus down more precisely to the world of hot rodding and I can relate a more immediate reaction to this world-wide pandemic and what effect if had on us as enthusiasts. Here in Australia the pandemic meant a complete stop to almost all forms of entertainment and sport, including automotive events, as whole areas were locked down at different times, even making it impossible to go to work for most people

for weeks at a time. Being a small, family owned publishing company located in regional Victoria meant the negative effects on us turned out to be quite minimal, in fact the COVID-19 pandemic even had several positive outcomes for us that we didn't anticipate. It seems that a great many hot rod and custom enthusiasts retreated into their workshops and reading rooms and went to work on their projects with renewed vigor – there wasn't much else we could do. But that retreat also meant information was needed and as a consequence our mail-order tech book service really ramped up – opposite to what we had expected. In situations like those presented by a COVID-19 pandemic, I am convinced that hot rodders fared better than most, not least because I believe the ability to throw yourself deep into a project has hidden mental health benefits at such a time.

I know that process is exactly what I experienced as I retreated into my home workshop and made great progress on my Model A Bucket re-creation project. Not only was that good for my own mental health, it also provided a host of technical articles for our Australian Street Rodding magazine at a time when we couldn't travel to gather our normal content of feature cars and events. You can see some other side benefits right here in this issue of Hot Rodding International in the form of retrospective articles developed from our extensive archives.

Surely, we can all look forward to adjusting back to a world with less COVID-19 related restrictions now that vaccines are being administered world-wide. I hope you didn't suffer badly through this pandemic and can now return to something near a normal lifestyle by doing the things you love with your old cars.

Waihi Beach, New Zealand JALOPY

The world might be crippled by COVID-19, but in New Zealand, the Jalopy Dust Up was a dusty but fun way to see in 2021. Hosted by Noddy Watts of Beach Hop fame (New Zealand's biggest hot rod, classic car and rock 'n' roll festival, see separate coverage beginning on page 48) and his partner Andrea, the Dust Up was just what the doctor ordered. Let's face it, 2020 in New Zealand consisted of two complete lock-downs, numerous cancelled or delayed car events and there's no doubt the Jalopy Dust up was a sure way to inject some low-key fun back into the hot rodding calendar.

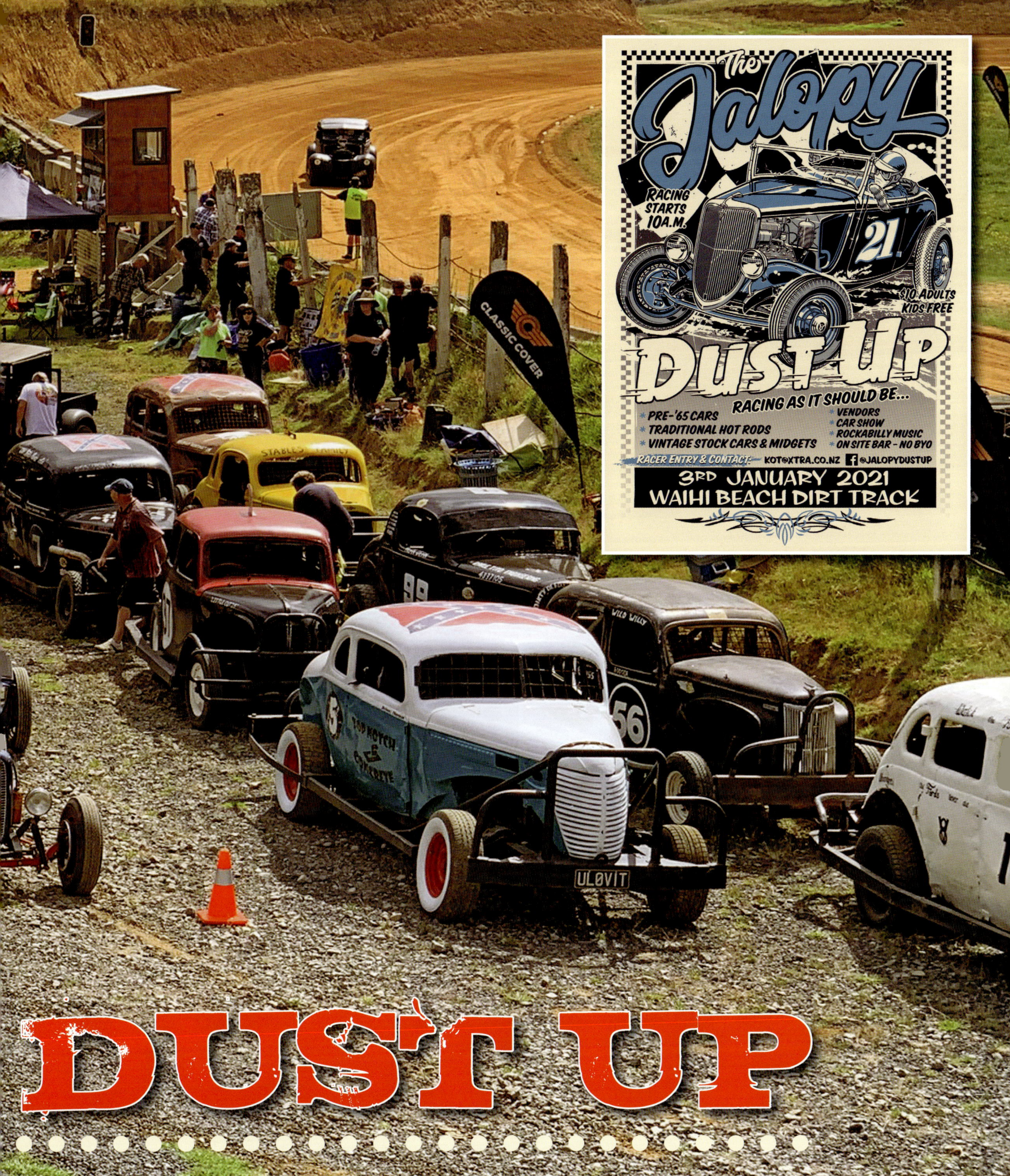

DUST UP

Based at the picturesque Waihi Beach Dirt Track, the Dust Up delivered a smorgasbord of pre 1965 style hot rods, vintage midgets and vintage stock cars. Held at the peak of the New Zealand summer, the weather was scorching and the racing was all just for fun from the standpoint of the participants or spectators. No prizes, no grand appearances, just good old fashioned dirt oval fun. For further information about what Noddy Watts does for the hot rod and classic car fraternity in New Zealand, check out the website: www.beachhop.co.nz or look up the Beach Hop or Kiwis on Tour on Facebook.

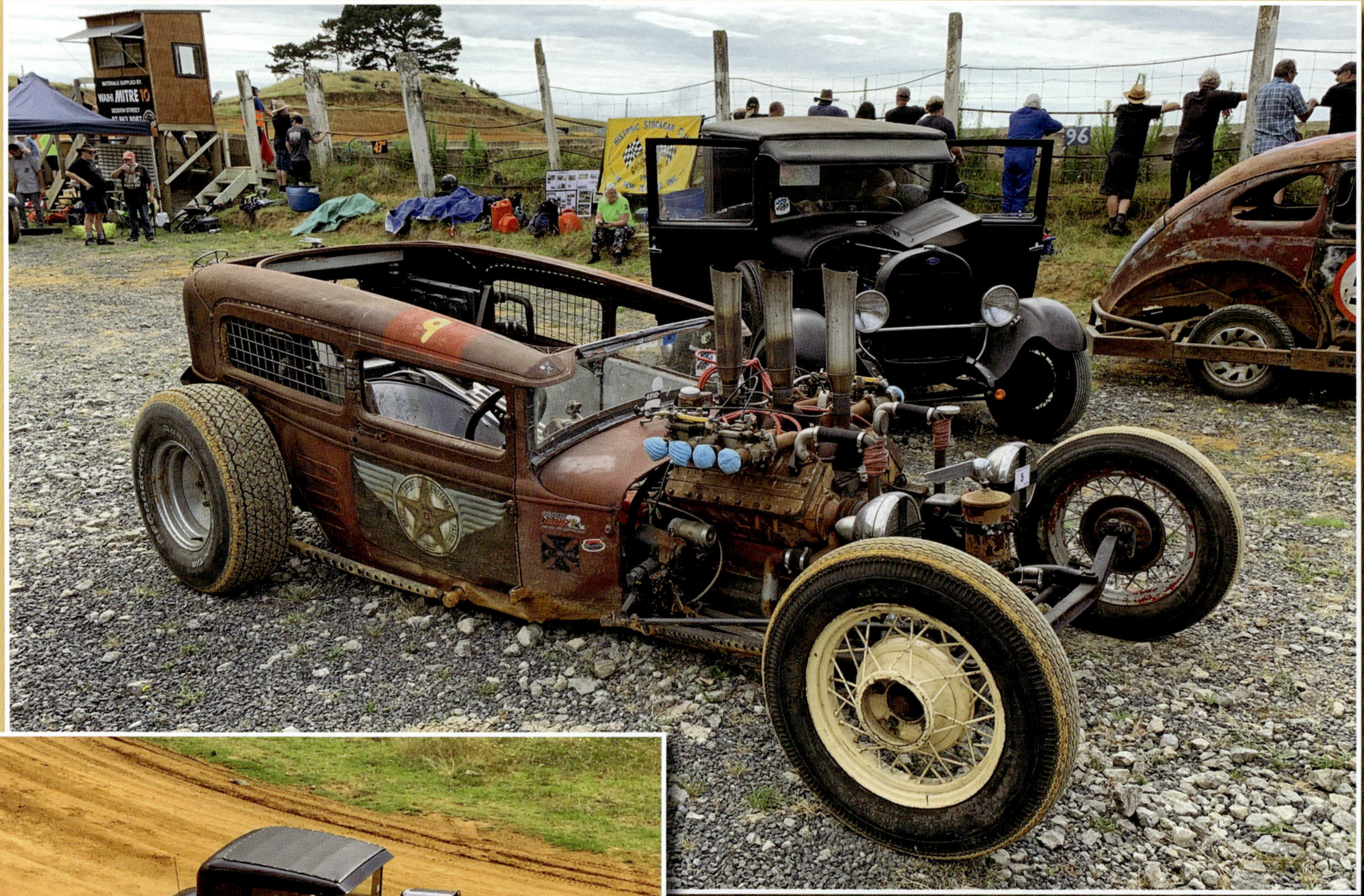

ABOVE: Neil Surtees' hydraulic hot rod is this chopped and channelled Model A Tudor on hydraulic suspension with a Caddy flathead V8.

LEFT: Notable road racing touring car driver, Dean Perkins pedalled this high horsepower blown Model A coupe with ease on the dirt and made it look all too easy!

ABOVE: The vintage stock cars were a real throwback in time. This would be the equivalent of California jalopy racing.

ABOVE: "Street Jalopies" wait patiently for their turn to throw up some dust on the Waihi dirt track circuit.

ABOVE RIGHT: Vintage stock cars in silhouette against the ocean, what a fine way to spend a summer day, post COVID-19 lockdown.

RIGHT: Banger powered Model A Ford pickups head up this group of would be race cars assembled in the pits.

ABOVE: Mike Courtney's Model A Ford based sprint car looks brand new for the 1935 speedway championship season, except that it's 2021 already! That's a readily recognisable Stromberg 97 carby hanging off the intake manifold of this period perfect sprint car.

JALOPY DUST UP

ABOVE: Jim Hanham's Model A roadster pickup runs a stout Hemi engine but Jim plays it cool and calm behind the wheel.

BELOW: Chris Hawkes is no stranger to going sideways having run road rallies with his '55 Chev pickup (that was cut down from a sedan).

MAIN: Demonstration runs by midget racers and vintage stock cars provided extra entertainment for the crowd at the Jalopy Dust Up.

ABOVE: Bruce Beaumont's '34 Ford five window coupe is basically a dirt oval hot rod with speedway suspension. Bruce's dirt oval experience enabled him to drive the car like a proper speedway car too.
LEFT: Brad Taylor in Dave Best's wooden spoke wheeled Durant speedster about to be overtaken by Mark Stokes in Greg's T roadster. Great fun!

ABOVE & RIGHT: Mike Wells of Whakatane, has had this Caddy powered '28 Model A roadster for over thirty years and in that time it has inspired many a young and upcoming hot rodder to take advantage of the affordable hot rod fun you can enjoy.

ABOVE: Roll up in your own "jalopy" and have some low-key racing fun, or just kick back under the shade of a tree and enjoy some summertime hot rodding entertainment.

ABOVE: HRI contributorr, Greg Stokes' 1922 Ford Model T roadster. You could still smell the brush painted black paint (by Greg's partner Tania) applied the night before. This was the result of a 10 day thrash commencing on Christmas Eve. Greg operates GMS Hot Rods in West Auckland and used the Christmas/New Year break to get his own project finished. It was a rolling body/chassis before he started the 10 day thrash where he was helped greatly by his Dad, Mark. Due to a spell of wet weather the day before the Jalopy Dust Up, the event was postponed by one day which gave Greg the "extra" day he needed to finish his thirties era "gow job" hot rod. Greg and his Dad Mark shared the driving duties throughout the day after toiling together to get the car finished in time.

RIGHT: The man responsible for the post COVID-19 hot rodding fun, Noddy Watts has been the promoter of Beach Hop since its inception and decided the Jalopy Dust Up would brighten up everyone's outlook. We agree!

MAIN: The Waihi Dirt Track overlooks the ocean and provides a spectacular venue for a fun-based event.

LEFT: Peter "PJ" Jenkins built this really timeless Model A coupe he sourced from the USA. A refreshing change is to see a painted and detailed factory appearing 327 Chev for power.

BELOW LEFT: Street cars wait their turn for a blast around the track while the stock car racers do their thing in the background.

BELOW: How about this robust truck rim based scattershield?

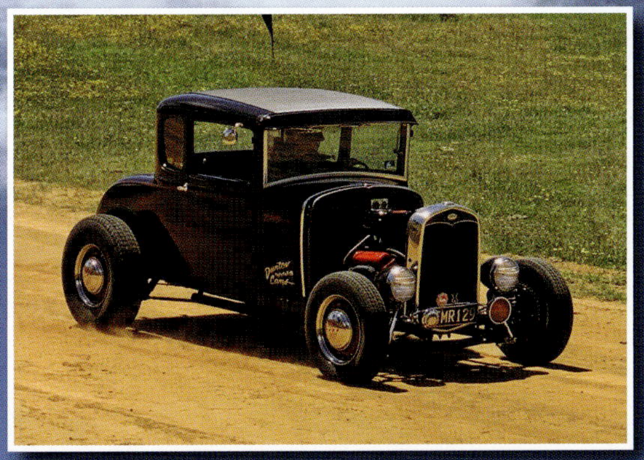

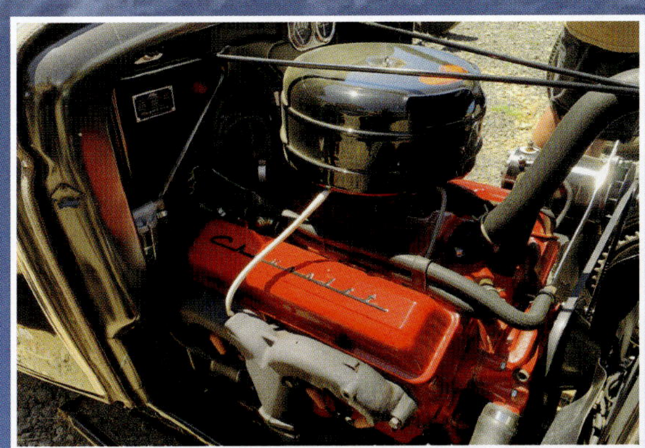

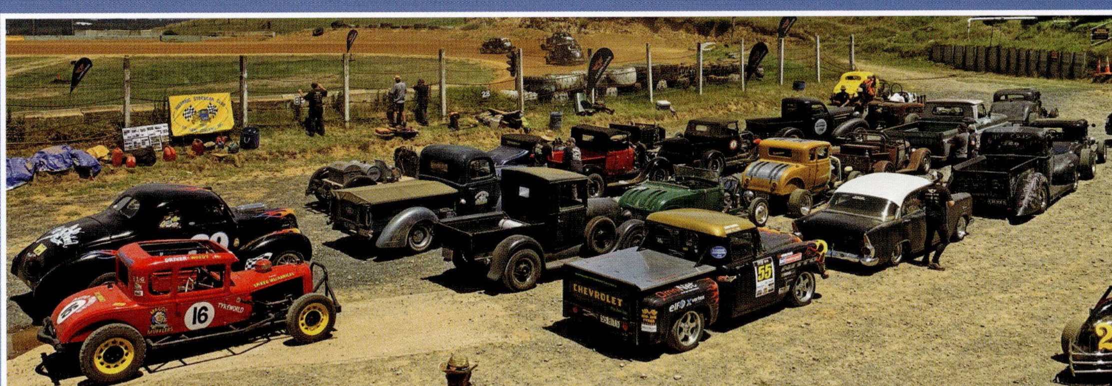

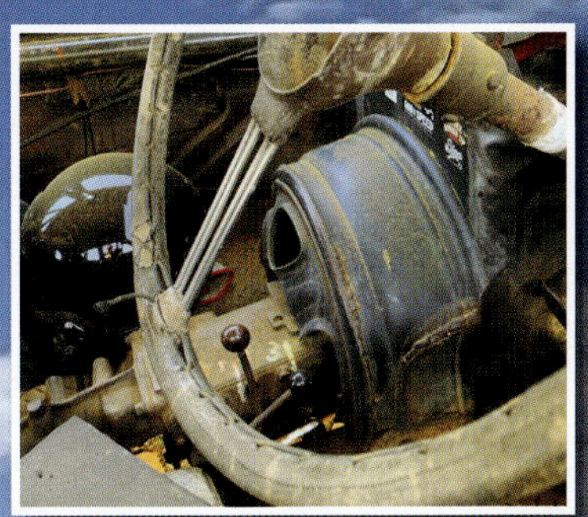

JALOPY DUST UP

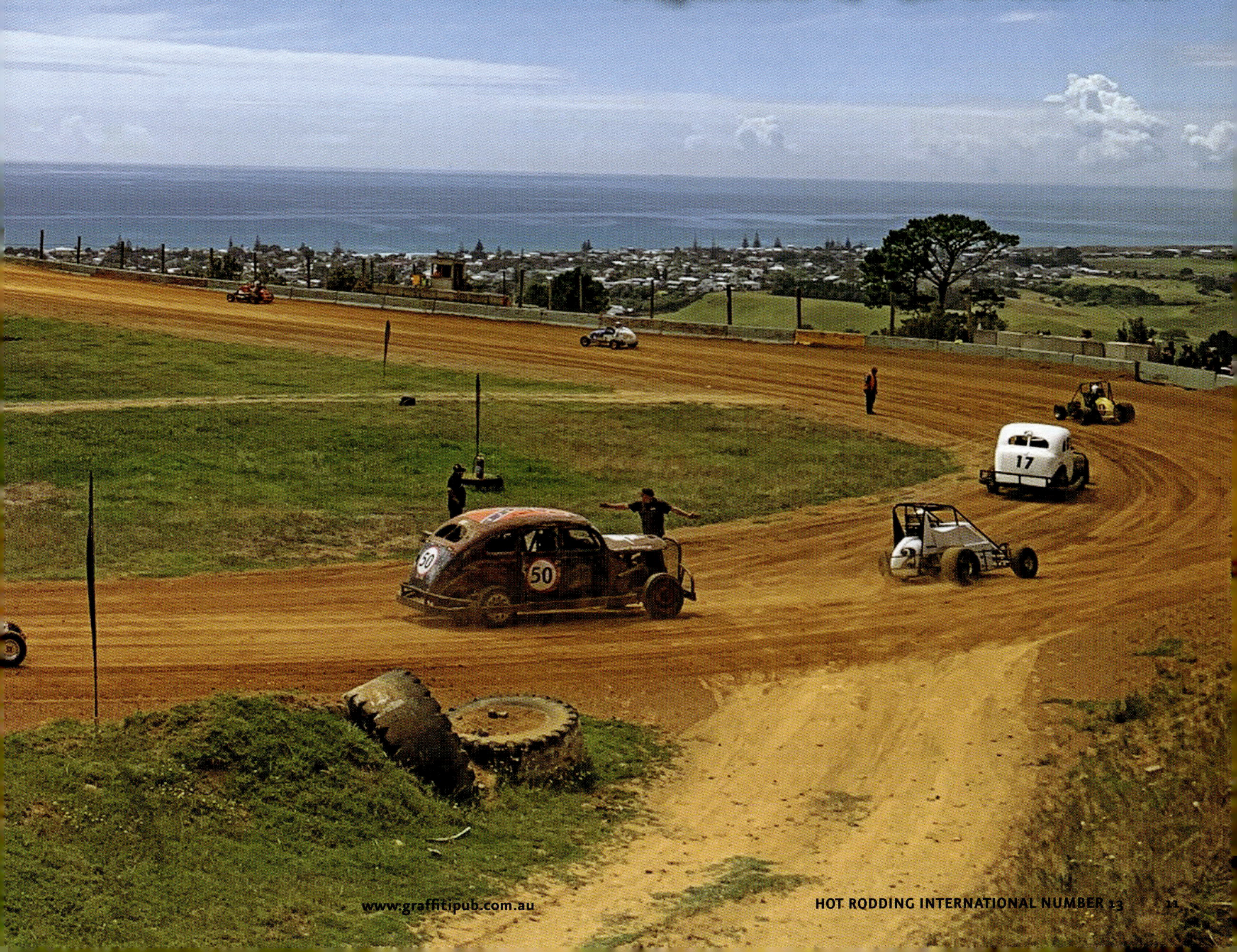

gallery

Stefan Marjoram
Animator, Film-Maker and Artist

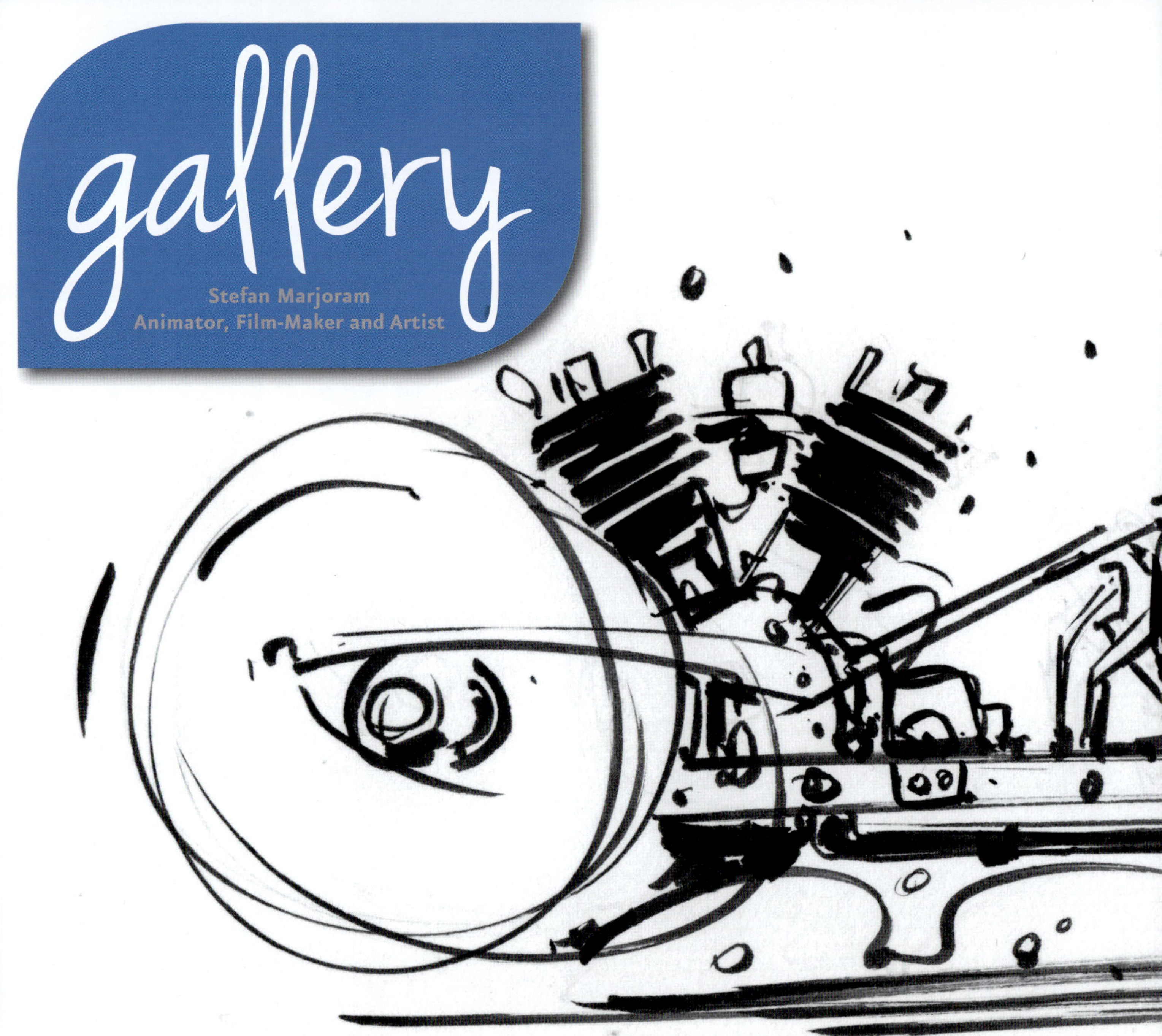

Artist, photographer and film maker, Stefan Marjoram is based in Somerset in the United Kingdom. He started his career in animation, directing short films and television idents - working for a long time in the Aardman studios (where they make Wallace and Gromit). Always a massive car nut, when Richard Noble moved in next door to start building his supersonic car Bloodhound. Stefan was straight over to offer his services as a photographer and artist, but it turned out they really needed a film-maker, so that they could share the amazing engineering story in an educational way. Stefan thought he could do a sabbatical for a year or two and ended up staying for eight! With recessions and Brexit (and now the Corona Virus) they couldn't have picked a harder time to take on such a massive project. It briefly went into administration and is now in the hands of an entrepreneur with a slightly cut-down team (that no longer includes Stefan). But he still follows the project closely, it's so close to being ready to set a record.

The car drawings are something that Stefan started doing seriously about 10 years ago. "I used to go to events and take a lot of photos. One day I thought I'd try some sketching. The cars proved an interesting challenge and I discovered that, although I ended up with fewer images, I had enjoyed the event that much more. Spending a weekend looking through a viewfinder can be quite antisocial, whereas sitting on a stool sketching for an hour you actually get to chat to people - it might be the owners or other spectators - lots of whom say they used to love sketching or would like to be able to do it. With this in mind I've started doing free drawing sessions for the Bugatti Trust during hill climb events."

The more Stefan learned about cars, the more he like the earlier models. Vintage cars and specials have such a lot of character – either from the artistry of the builder – or from years of competition – or both. They make great drawing subjects - and hot rods fit perfectly into that category. Each one is unique. "I really like how the art

scene is such a huge part of hot rodding culture too. There aren't masses of hot rod events around me, but the VHRA more than makes up for it. A super dedicated group with the coolest cars, every event is special. A few years back they managed to organise an event on Pendine Sands (our Bonneville in the 1920s) and to see vintage machines in such a timeless and historic setting is really magical."

As you can see from the drawings Stefan mostly likes to work from life. For tools he often uses pencil and watercolour, sometimes a sharpie if he's getting too "tight" and increasingly an iPad. "They'e all just tools and I like the way they change your drawing style. The bonus with the iPad is that you can output a time-lapse and see the drawing appear line by line – something that has proved very popular with big manufacturers like Ferrari – who are looking for ways to pep up their Instagram feeds.

Occasionally I'll get asked to do commissions from photos and in the winter when there are fewer events I have to turn to my imagination - and these drawings often have a slightly cartoony feel. I have no interest in simply reproducing a photo."

When he's not drawing hot rods Stefan is usually drawing vintage cars. It's a huge scene in the UK and he finds himself surrounded by venues, garages and owners, including the rebuilding of the Beast of Turin record car – which made an interesting contrast to Bloodhound. Some of the most interesting cars in the VSCC are hill-climb specials that Stefan regards as the British hot rod. They would take a spindly cyclecar chassis and drop in an aero engine or a big bike engine. A few hastily riveted aluminium panels and they were ready to race. With thin wheels and too much power, these oil covered, chain-driven contraptions slide their way up the hill, making the best noises (and smells). "I am truly indebted to the eccentric group who build and race these cars (and sometimes even take me as a passenger) - they're truly inspiring" – Stefan.

■

ABOVE: If the Blues Brothers were set in th 1930s. Part of the 2017 Advent series.

BELOW: Quick pencil thumbnails done as the cars queued to go up the hill at GOW! Prescott.

ABOVE: Built by Leslie Ballamy in 1937, this Ford special features independent front suspension.

RIGHT: One of my favourite cars of the VHRA. I love the simplicity of the Model T.

BELOW: I made a very loose iPad sketch of this car in the paddock and decided when I got home to give it a cartoon feel.

BELOW RIGHT: An "English Hot Rod" - built in the 1920s.

ABOVE: This was a recent commission - the postal truck had such a lot of character. I thought it would be fun to tell a bit of a story.
ABOVE RIGHT: Done in the paddock at Prescott - one of my favourite sketches - why don't they all come out like this?
BELOW: The GN Thunderbug is a modern day vintage special. Built using pre 1931 parts it has a thumping great 4.3 litre v-twin.

ABOVE: If the Ghostbusters drove a Model T - part of the 2017 Advent series.
BELOW: I sketched this car built by Frenchman Christophe Mehault at the VHRA meet on Pendine Sands - the first time I'd seen a streamliner.

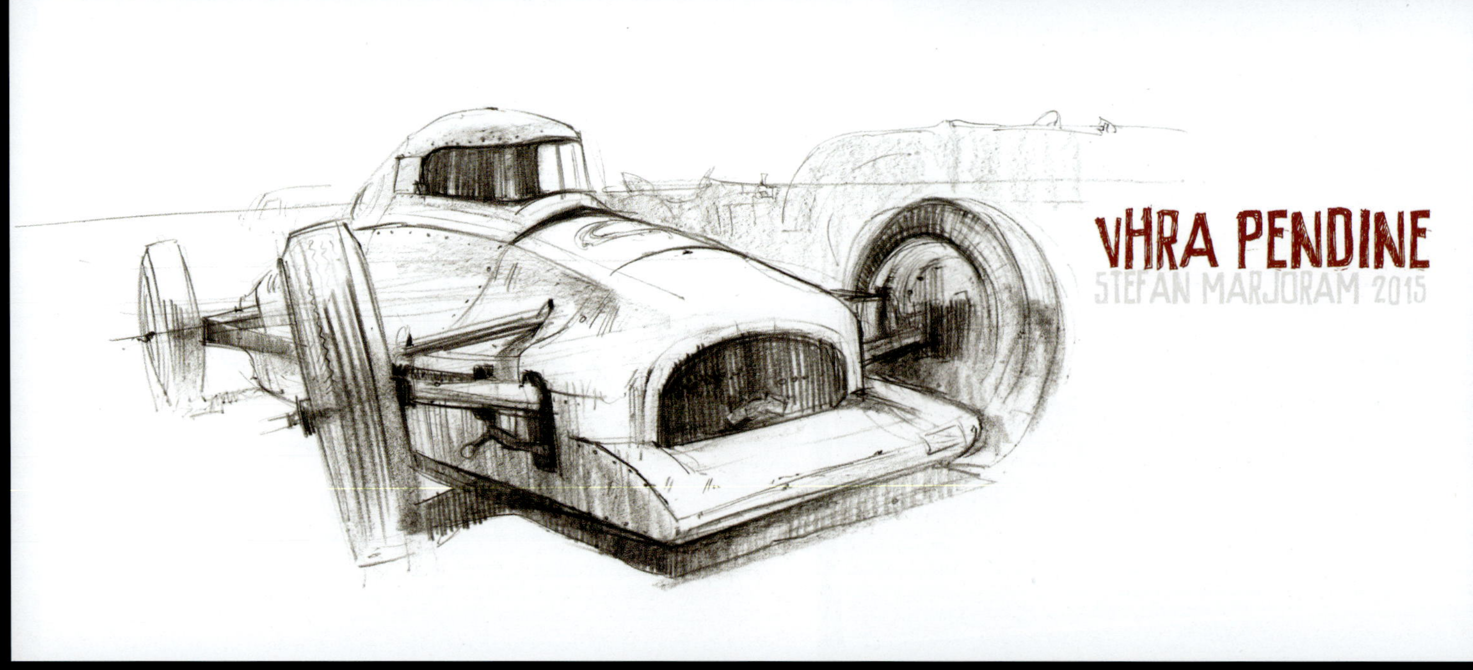

ABOVE: Another commission. I'm looking forward to one day seeing "Old Red" in person.

BELOW: A pickup waits for the tide to recede - revealing the pristine Pendine track.

RIGHT: Another from the 2017 Advent series. This time it's vintage Starsky and Hutch.

BELOW: The amazing 1911 "Golden Ford" is a genuine Brooklands racer.

BOTTOM: Occasionally I find I'm getting too fussy with the pencils and it's time to be brave and use a Sharpie.

ABOVE: GOW coupe

ABOVE: Time at Pendine is limited by the tide and there's so much to see. Sometimes thumbnail sketches are the quickest way to capture everything.

BELOW: A quick birthday doodle for a friend. The car is a VSCC special called "The Hornet" and is powered by a pair of vintage Harley engines. The plan was to up it to four engines one day!

ABOVE: Once the cars are off the beach and everyone's sharing stories in the pub, I can sit and draw a few cars without having to hurry. This Oldsmobile police car was something a bit different.

RIGHT: This lovely Bobtail T was at one of the VSCC events at Prescott – quite a rare car car over here.

Ford 'Bobtail T'

ABOVE: Hot rods are a joy to draw – particularly the more extreme ones.

RIGHT: 2017 Advent - If the Good Old Boys were hot rodders.

TOP LEFT: December 2018 was quite busy for me. A brush-pen made the daily Advent drawings much quicker to do. I also invented stories to go with the pictures – which fooled quite a few people!

TOP RIGHT: Miller Golden Submarine.

ABOVE: In 2016 the Advent series featured some of my favourite cars - including Clayton Paddison's perfect Model T.

ABOVE: Once a year the VHRA book Prescott Hill Climb for their very own event. It's an amazing setting and very laid back – perfect for sketching.

LEFT: Modern iPads are very similar to pencil and paper for sketching. Having layers makes it a lot easier to experiment with colour.

DLRA Aussie Dry Lakes Racing

RIGHT: A party of American racers brought their vehicles to Lake Gairdner in 1995 to take part in Speed Week with the Aussie racers. None were more outstanding than veteran salt lake racer Al Teague whose finger-like streamliner was the fastest on the American scene for many years.

BELOW: Al Teague sits in the driver's cockpit as the crew prepares for another run down the Lake Gairdner salt. Damp spots on the surface of the lake that year hampered performance but Al still posted the top speed of the meet at 366 mph.

The First Decade

The Dry Lakes Racers Australia annual speed trials was to celebrate its 30th anniversary with its 2020 Speed Week meeting, but alas, it had to be cancelled at the last minute due to COVID-19 restrictions. Coverage of the 2020 DLRA Speed Week, that has been held at Lake Gairdner in the South Australian outback since 1990 would have been featured in this issue of Hot Rodding International. Rather than drop coverage altogether we decided to use that 30th anniversary as the basis for a look back at the first decade of Australian salt lake racing in this article. It's amazing how quickly the DLRA Speed Week has become a feature of the auto racing scene downunder.

Our own archive of DLRA Speed Week coverages (over 10,400 photos) contains many unpublished images from that first decade of racing so we have selected a clutch of them for this historical restrospective.

Over the 30 years there have often been extremely good salt conditions, a few not so good, and thankfully only a very few total wash-outs. Lake Gairdner truly is a slice of salt lake racing paradise. ■

Words: Larry O'Toole,
Photos: Graffiti Archive

ABOVE: Check the specially made decal on the front of Al Teague's streamliner celebrating the Australian International Land Speed Salt Flat Challenge 1995.
BELOW: The DLRA logo has been in use since the organisation got under way officially in 1985.

DLRA - The First Decade

www.graffitipub.com.au

LEFT: Inaugural President of the DLRA and devoted salt lake racer Mike Davidson campaigned this blown flathead powered T roadster, over several years it improved from 129 mph all the way up to a best speed of 176 mph. The supercharged flathead engine used reworked Kong heads and much of Davidson's own flathead building expertise that he developed in his own workshop over many years.

ABOVE: One of the most impressive looking cars to ever run at Lake Gairdner was the Rea, Weir & Mumford T roadster, shown here at the 1999 meet being pushed by Geoff Rea's street Deuce coupe. Wayne Mumford posted the fastest speed for the team that year at 143.027mph. The T roadster ran an injected flathead engine for most of the early meets but for one meet was fitted with American racer, Chuck Sharpe's four banger Ford engine (top photo with "Sharpe" sign added to the engine hood). Chuck sent the engine out earlier, then flew out to drive the car at the 2001 Speed Week meeting. He was 72 years of age at the time and is still actively building four banger engines today at the age of 91!

LEFT: Chris Weir waits patiently in the T roadster for his turn to move up to the start line while Wayne Mumford reminds us all where this is taking place by holding a DLRA Lake Gairdner sign. The T roadster has been retired for some years now but will always remain a favourite in the memory of regular visitors to the DLRA Lake Gairdner Speed Week trials.

TOP: Leigh Fielder purchased the Pontiac Trans-Am from the USA and re-equipped it to run at Lake Gairdner, clocking 211.50 mph. Leigh also took the car back to Bonneville where it succeeded in breaking an SCTA record.

ABOVE: Californian four banger Ford hot rodder, Chuck Sharpe poses with Judy McAllister's Model T roadster pickup. Chuck raced at Lake Gairdner in 1995 then again in 2001 and 2002, posting a top run of 122.050 mph with his own four banger early Ford motor in the Rea, Weir and Mumford T roadster.

TOP: The blue '46 Studebaker pickup of Craig Parsons ran 103.96 mph using 259 cubic inch Studebaker V8 running gear in 1995.

ABOVE: The Moe Boys campaigned their yellow XA Falcon coupe for many of the early years and recently brought it out of retirement.

MAIN PIC: A dark storm over the salt is an impressive sight. This the 1999 event and shows Ray Charlton's 1932 Ford roadster and John Lynch's belly tank tucked away, patiently waiting for the weather to clear up so that racing could resume.

DLRA - The First Decade

TOP: Lee Russell drove his Suzuki from Queensland with a tiny 561 cc race engine bolted in place of the passenger seat, changed it on arrival and went nearly 20 mph faster than the Bonneville record for his class!

ABOVE: Ray Charlton's small block Chevy powered 1932 Ford roadster being checked out by Peter Gregory and Wally James. The photo was taken at the 1998 meet where Ray got his hot rod up to 153.326 mph. At a later meeting Ray got the roadster to almost 180 mph and then retired from racing.

TOP: Norm Hardinge and Vicki Howard were introduced to salt lake racing in their satin black FJ Holden ute in 1999 and Norm has been a regular competitor ever since. On this occasion Vicki actually went slightly faster than Norm at 112.240 mph.

ABOVE: This XA GT Ford Falcon from Club Animal Racing made improvements on every run at the 1998 event. It was running a 351 Cleveland and eventually went 162.339 mph with Steve "Animal" Charlton driving.

DLRA - The First Decade

TOP INSET: Few competitors have put as much into the DLRA Speed Week as Rod Hadfield. This big block Chevy powered Studebaker replaced the Salt Shaker Lakester when it was retired.

ABOVE: The Salt Shaker started life as The Proud Australian top fuel dragster that was driven by Ross Mellish on Australian drag strips. Rod converted it for salt lake racing, was lucky to survive a horrendous crash in 1991 (see below) and then rebuilt it to compete again. The Salt Shaker now resides in Rod's Hadfield's personal museum in Castlemaine.

OPPOSITE PAGE TOP: Rod Hadfield also ran his hiboy Model A roadster at the salt lake with a few modifications to convert it from drag racing duties. Note the large diameter aircraft tyres on the rear in the first picture. Rod complained of the car not responding as expected with these tyres and "hitting the wall" at 151 mph on each run. A suggestion to try running the smaller diameter wheels and tyres off brother, Mark's Mustang (right photo) saw the roadster immediately improve to 168 mph and really test its engineering for such high speeds. It was returned to nostalgia drag racing duties while Rod went on to race at the salt in his Salt Shaker lakester, orange Studebaker and the Bronze Aussie Commodore.

OPPOSITE PAGE CENTRE Rod's brother, Mark Hadfield had his share of racing troubles at the 1991 meet. During one run the bonnet scoop came off in spectacular fashion while on another high speed run the whole bonnet of his red, 302 Windsor powered '65 Mustang Fastback broke its restraints and flipped over, smashing the windscreen and severely denting the roof. Top speed for this meet was 152.82 mph. Mark restored the Mustang and it now only sees street duty.

OPPOSITE PAGE BOTTOM: Mark Hadfield then teamed up with Wally James and returned in a race only '67 Mustang that went 179.104 mph in 2002 using a Boss 302 Ford V8 engine. The Mustang is now a restored street car.

ABOVE: The result of barrel-rolling a lakester at speed. Rod Hadfield was very lucky to survive this horrific crash in 1991. He broke both of his wrists in this accident and is being attended to by the paramedic under the shade awning in the background of this photo while awaiting the arrival of the Royal Flying Doctor plane that air-lifted him to the Port Augusta Hospital. Rod rebuilt this car with a big block Chevy motor and returned to Lake Gairdner with it in 1994.

The Castlemaine Kid

44

CASTLE ELECTRICS & EXHAUSTS
Mark Hadfield
Roy Charlton
SPECIAL INTEREST AUTO'S
D PROD 67
302 ci
BJ Ginnivan
SALT·67

ABOVE: John Lynch's bellytank Lakester always had a presence at the lake, right from when it first appeared in 1995 in this guise. The vehicle was constructed in Castlemaine and used a hand made alloy "tank" body and blown Keith Black Hemi engine prepared by Al Teague.

ABOVE & BELOW: A scalloped paint scheme was added to John Lynch's bellytank after its first appearance and he came back several more times, gradually increasing speeds from 200 mph all the way up to a best of 301 mph, that still stands as the fastest speed by an Australian competitor in an Australian built vehicle. Kiwi crew member, John Marshall looks on from directly behind as John heads out for a run on the "warm-up" track and spectators get a close up opportunity to absorb the scene above. Watching this machine run at 300 mph was an awesome experience.

LEFT: Garth Butterworth's XP Falcon ute with hand-painted signwriting and roof mounted aerials was used as the DLRA "Official Timing Vehicle" in 1991.

RIGHT: Rob Carroll's '32 Ford roadster is 351 V8 Ford Windsor powered. The historic roadster has since returned to street duties only. Rob's roadster was originally a channelled version that was a regular competitor at Riverside Drags in Melbourne when owned by Rip Kirby. Rob served several terms as DLRA President.

ABOVE: Bob Bowman and his crew ran this T Ford roadster in 1998 with Teamspeed sponsorship. Peter Watson ran it the fastest at 155.783 mph, Dick Bushell went 146.980 mph and Bowman wasn't far behind, posting a best run at 147.657 mph. The T roadster has been a regular competitor at Lake Gairdner right up until now.

LEFT: The red '27 Chevy roadster of Paul Greaves and Jeremy Nunn looked impressive and ran a top speed of 134.35 mph with Nunn behind the wheel in 1995.

DLRA - The First Decade

TOP: Bob Bowman watches on as the crew deal with the parachute after returning from another run in the T roadster. The T first competed at the 1998 meeting and has been there every time since.

RIGHT: Graeme Holden's red '53 Ford Vicky retained its 239 flathead powerplant to haul the heavy package to a best speed of 97.06 mph at Speed Week in 1993.

BELOW: Richard Hollywood brought his XM Falcon hardtop over from New Zealand on several occasions and it was a solid performer for the time.

BELOW LEFT: American hot rodding legend, the late Tex Smith came out to Lake Gairdner several times and also loved fishing and a cheeky joke. We've published this 1999 photo of him "fishing" before but it's a gem. He's using a tent pole and bungee cord while the "hole in the "ice" is actually just a plastic bag.

ABOVE: Keith Stamp's Deuce coupe ran its best speed in 1999 at 138.846 mph. He is shown at left above sharing some banter with the late Tex Smith. Watching on in the background is regular DLRA competitor, Mark Dunn.

LEFT: Tony Cassar thrashed this '34 Ford three window coupe together in just three months to get it to its one and only meet in 1994. Running a quad-carb and Waggott head equipped flathead, Tony ran his chopped coupe to a top speed of 85.09 mph.

TOP: American, Chuck Salmen brought his "$um Fun" '34 Ford roadster out to Australia three times between 1995 and 2000. The roadster regularly ran over 250 mph.

ABOVE LEFT: Front wheel drive was a feature of the tear-drop shaped streamliner of the Walkey Bros, one of the visiting American racers in 1995.

ABOVE RIGHT: Elongated Simca coupe belonging to another of the American racers, George Fields was billed as the world's fastest coupe in 1995. It ran a 470 cubic inch blown Hemi but was plagued with mechanical problems and couldn't perform to its full potential.

ABOVE: Kevin Saville's low-slung '27 Model T roadster was a solid performer on the salt and achieved its best run in 1995 with a 184.27 mph pass – outstanding for a blown Holden six cylinder engine.

LEFT: Kevin Saville and his pit crew prepare to unload the Holden powered T bucket after the dusty drive in from Iron Knob.

LEFT: Even the officials have time for a little tongue-in-cheek humour during Speed Week at Lake Gairdner.

RIGHT: Lucky Kaiser brought his Merlin powered bellytank bike to Lake Gairdner in the hope of securing a world record speed, but many attempts came up well short. The engine was two cylinders cut from a V12 Merlin. A change to a 302 Ford Cleveland V8 engine did see the bike eventually exceed 200 mph.

BELOW: All hands on deck to get Rob Carroll's tender truck out of a soft patch of salt in 1993. Racing conditions have varied over the years but have mostly been very good.

FAR LEFT: Hmmm, unidentified racers from an early period brought a hire car to the salt and applied a few tricks to get it close to 140 mph before returning it. They were politely told not to do that again!

LEFT & BELOW: Frank "Flatout" Robinson receives his trophy for Top Time of the Meet in 1993. His Model A roadster ran 140.26 mph on slushy salt.

BELOW: Lindsay Wilson's orange FX Holden ute really stands out against the pure white salt. In 1993 the humpy ute clocked a top speed of 101.31 mph.

ABOVE: In 1993, Neil Raymond ran his 1928 Model A Ford roadster pickup in the Blown Gas Modified Roadster category and set a record at 96.59 mph pass. He ran 120 mph in 1991 in a different class and returned in 1993, 1994 and 1995, improving each time, ending up with a best run of 174.10 mph.

BELOW: John Vevers had sponsorship from BP for an attempt on the world motorcycle record but didn't succeed.

ABOVE: Cameraman Tony Paterson uses Neil Raymond's pickup as a camera car in 1993 for some "on the move filming".
BELOW: Mike Bowden ran his 1950 Ford ute to 132.69 mph in 1995. He later sold the blown single spinner and recently bought it back after many years.
BELOW LEFT: Victorian hot rodder, Alan Murchison travelled out to Lake Gairdner in 1994 with this tri-powered flathead motivated '27 track T roadster, towed from Geelong by his mint 1955 Ford Customline wagon. Mechanical problems restricted the T to a best run of 86.41 mph but in 1999 it ran 131.338 mph with a tunnel ram equipped 351 Cleveland in the engine bay.

DLRA - The First Decade

BELOW: The Mt Ive homestead was used as a base when Lake Gairdner was being scoped out as a possible salt lake racing venue.

BELOW RIGHT: Motorcycles have dominated the entry numbers in recent years but in the early days there weren't so many. One of the most consistent bike racers over those years is Peter Vasittart on his Triumph.

BELOW: John Dent and Norm Bradshaw raced John's classic Mustang at first and have since progressed to their own individual 200+ mph racers. Norm is currently president of the DLRA. In the background is the Narrogin Boys "brick-like" XE Falcon from WA that regularly ran over 200 mph.

ABOVE: Getting to Lake Gairdner in the early days was an adventure in itself and spectator crowds weren't large as result, but all who made the trek vowed it was high on their bucket list. The experience of just standing on such a huge expanse of white salt makes the trip worthwhile on its own, but add in seeing racers test their machines to the upper limits is truly a unique experience.

LEFT: An engine swap for American racers the Walkey Bros in 1995 when five American crews shipped their vehicles to Lake Gairdner to try out the Aussie salt. The logistics exercise was mammoth as a large contigent of spectators came with them and travelled to the lake by bus where everything was shipped in and laid on for them. Fibreglass body manufacturer, Dick Williams was the main organiser of the huge international undertaking.

ABOVE: Heading for the start line in 1993. The '34 Ford cabriolet at the rear of the line was raced by Gary Tate. In front of it is the Rea/Weir/Mumfrod T roadster and in front of that again is Rob Carroll's '32 Ford hiboy roadster.

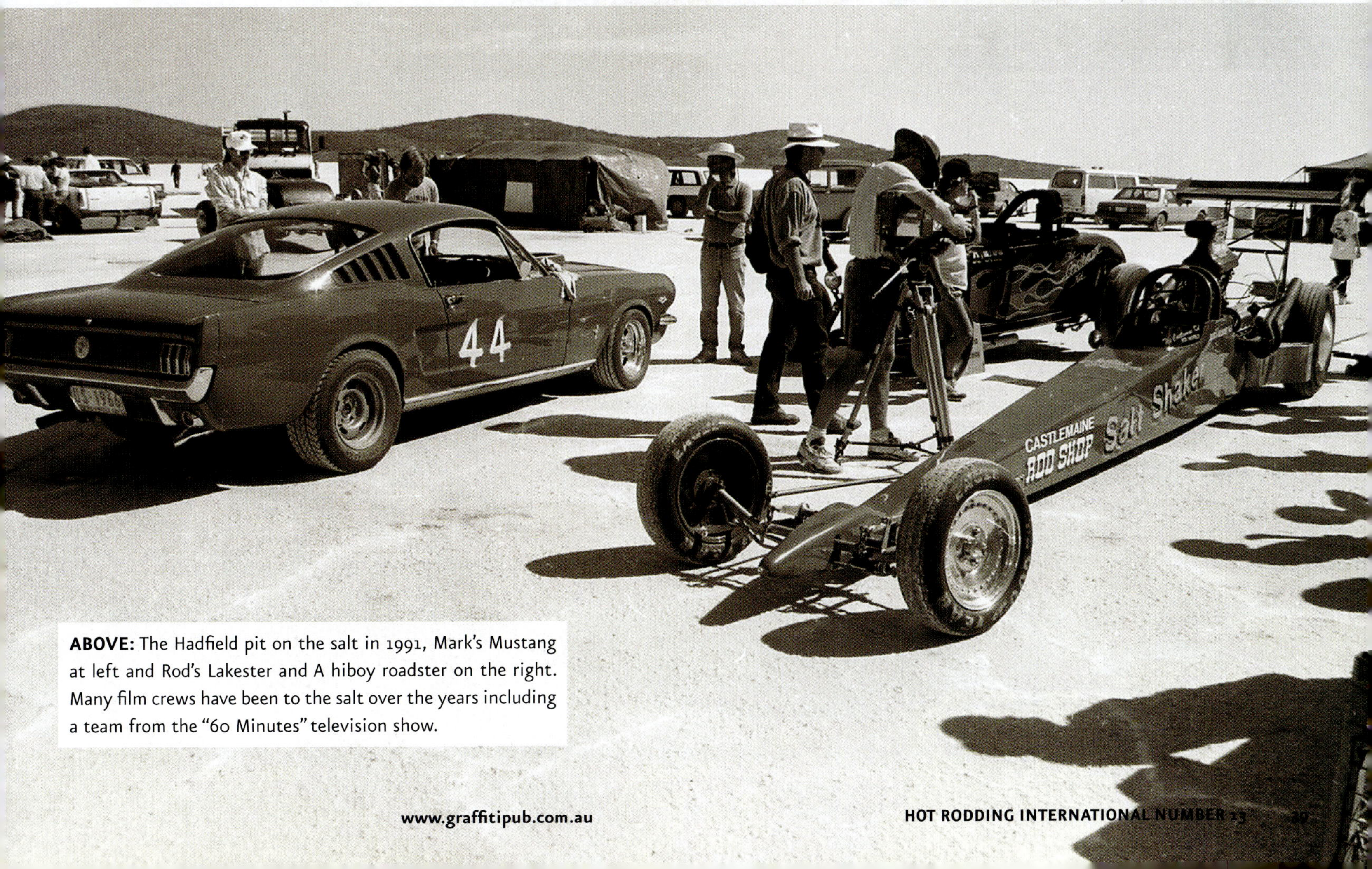

ABOVE: The Hadfield pit on the salt in 1991, Mark's Mustang at left and Rod's Lakester and A hiboy roadster on the right. Many film crews have been to the salt over the years including a team from the "60 Minutes" television show.

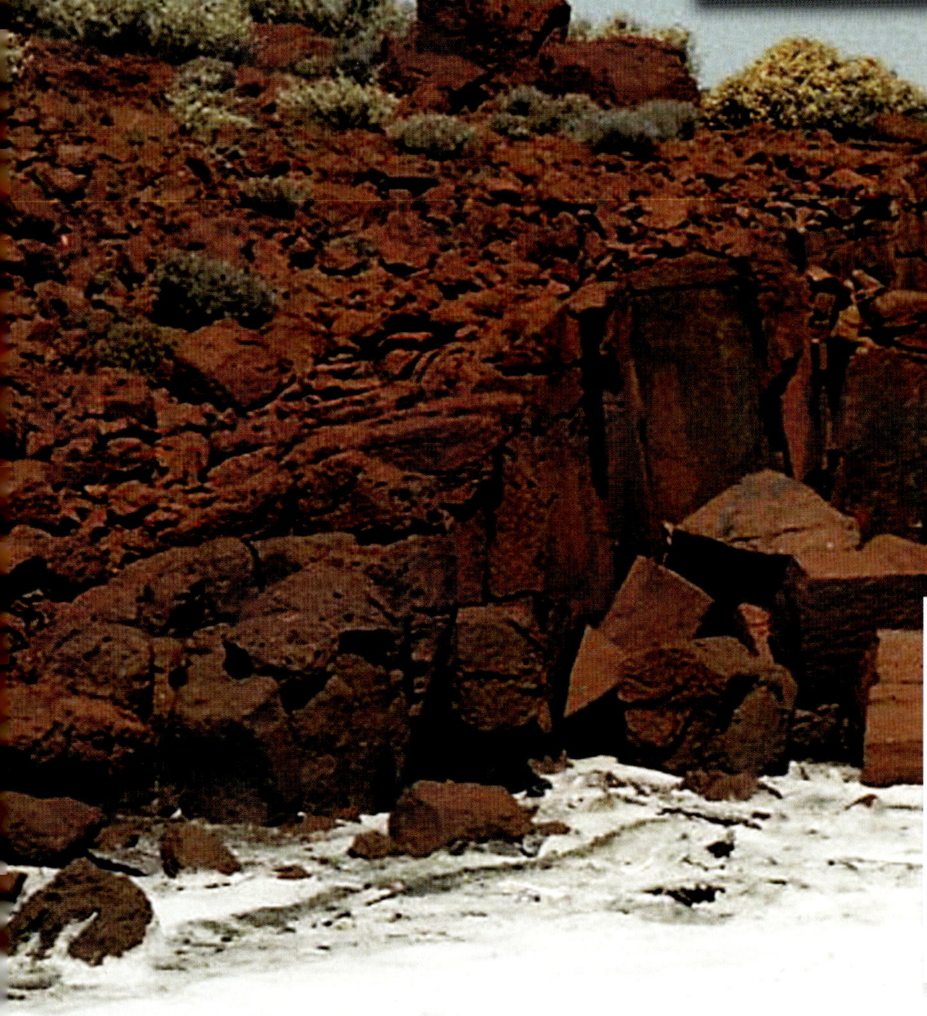

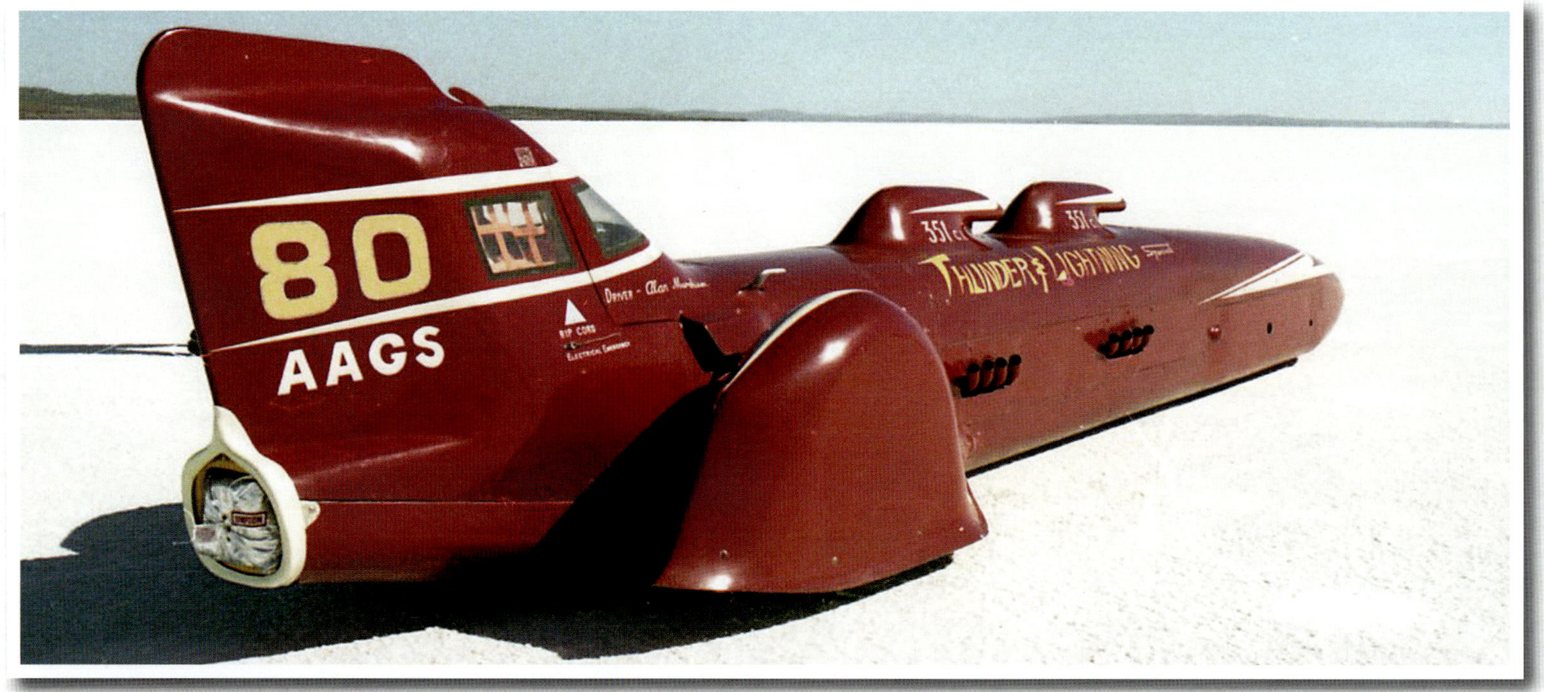

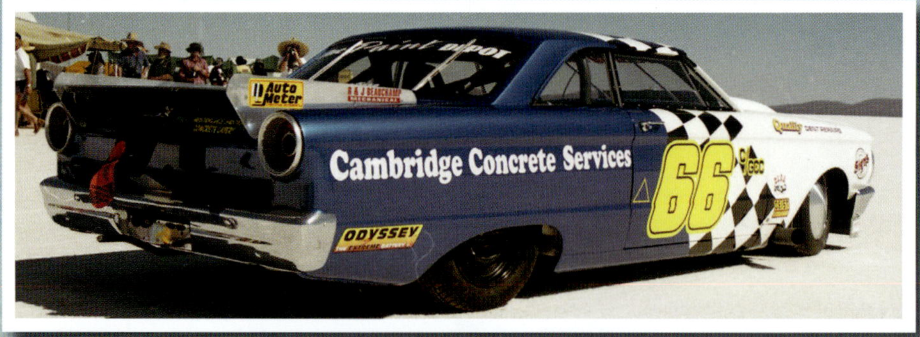
Auto Meter
Cambridge Concrete Services
66
ODYSSEY

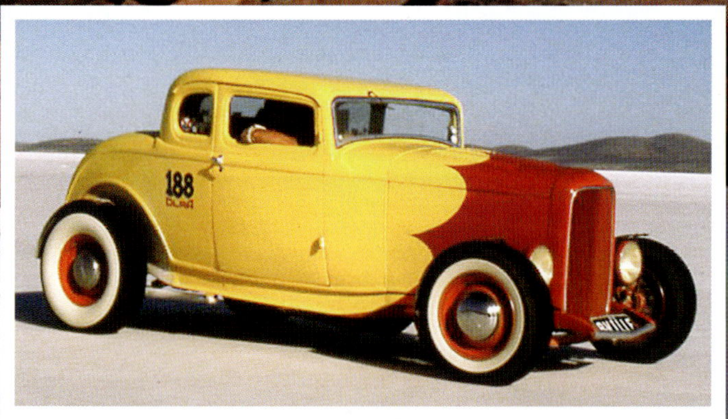
188

80
AAGS
THUNDER & LIGHTNING

TOP: Bob Ellis' XP hardtop racer shows a stark difference in profile to its push vehicle XP ute. The sleek Falcon ran better each year and topped 204 mph in 2005. These days Bob spends most of his time at Lake Gairdner as a racing official for the DLRA and he regularly assists with tech inspections at Bonneville Speed Week in the USA.

ABOVE: Mark Dunn campaigned his Holden station wagon for several years before stepping up to the current family lakester. The wagon ran a top speed of 163.882 mph on debut in 2002. Son, Kurt, only a lad in this picture, now regularly drives the lakester with dad, sister Gemma and more recently, Top Fuel drag racer Rachelle Splatt.

ABOVE LEFT: Geoff Rea drove his street registered Deuce coupe to the lake many times in the early years and then put it to work as the push car for the Rea/Weir/Mumford T racer before driving all the way back home to Gippsland in Victoria.

LEFT: One of the legends of Aussie salt lake racing is Alan Murchison who built and raced this wild twin engine streamliner in 2002. Running two Ford Cleveland engines, Alan coaxed them to 177.252 mph in 2002 before retiring from racing. Alan, from Barwon Heads in Victoria, has been involved in hot rodding since the 1950s.

MAIN PIC: The contrasts of Lake Gairdner are perfectly illustrated in this photo showing the red stone (full of iron) that encircles the pure white salt lake. Even if you aren't a salt lake racing enthusiast its an amazing place to visit.

HOT RODDITIES

It's one thing to attend large scale hot rodding events like the NSRA Street Rod Nationals to take in the thousands of rods on display, but it is also fun to soak up the atmosphere that goes along with activities at such events. Often you will stumble upon something that will take your breath away, or make you smile wryly because someone has done something that appeals to your sense of fun. Quirkiness makes the world go round and you won't find people more quirky than hot rodders out to have some fun.

Hence the subject of this article – "Hot Roddities", a collection of things that just popped up before our cameras while scouting around hot rodding events all over the world. These are just a few that have provided amusement, inspiration or just exhibit a genuine sense of fun. ■

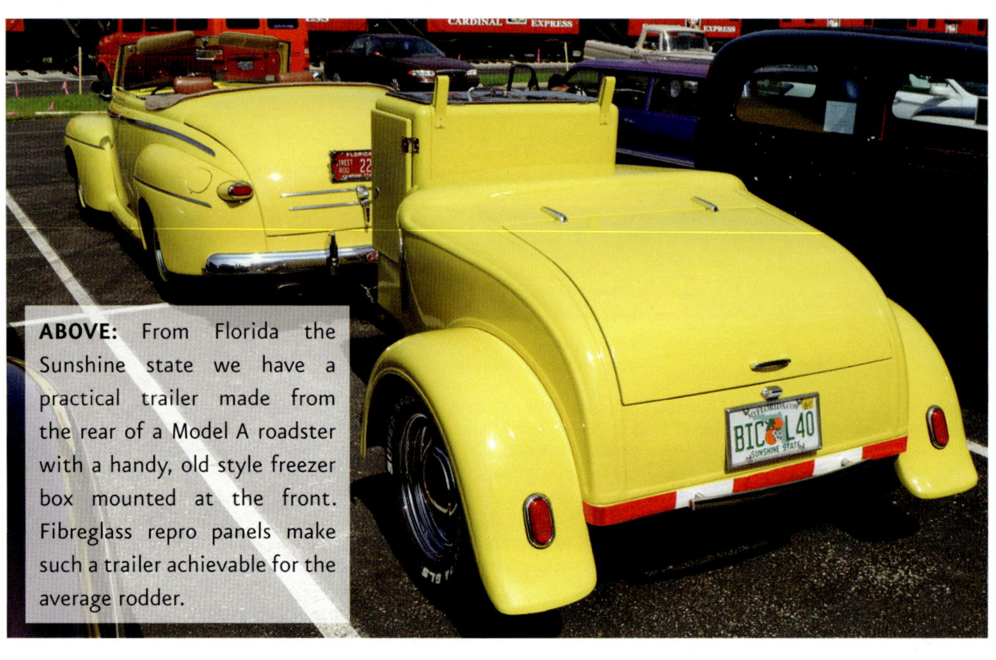

ABOVE: From Florida the Sunshine state we have a practical trailer made from the rear of a Model A roadster with a handy, old style freezer box mounted at the front. Fibreglass repro panels make such a trailer achievable for the average rodder.

ABOVE: T shirt from Bonneville makes its own statement, belongs to a crew of college students building a streamliner.

ABOVE & LEFT: You could be forgiven for not realising at first glance that this Model A coupe isn't the real deal. It's actually a very well proportioned mini-rod that's only about one third the size of a Model A Ford. "Childs Play" was on display at the UK Street Rod Supernationals in 2018 at Old Warden.

ABOVE: These two appear to be straight out of the Jetsons TV show and belong to Brent Mills. The white with blue top version is a one-off concept car known as a '59 Zar Car, the other a 1972 Electra King.

LEFT & BELOW: These rodders take matching outfits to the next level with their T bucket style trailer decked out in matching flamed finish to the roadster pulling it. This trailer even has its own "engine", actually a handy ice chest for the refreshments.

LEFT: 1900 Overland Custom. Built by lengendary customizer George Barris, the 1900 Overland covered wagon manure spreader was a gag gift from comedian Bob Hope to actor John Wayne on the occasion of his birthday. The custom wagon sat in a barn on John Wayne's estate until his death. A subsequent owner restored it and added disc brakes and seat belts. It is powered by a small-block Chevy V8. The wagon is in the collection of the Petersen Automotive Museum. Gift of Morad, Kambiz and Michael Zarabi.

RIGHT & BELOW: Where else but Bonneville would you expect to find bellytank racers – but maybe not this small? Beautifully executed mini-tanks were on display outside the Golden Nugget Casino where the rodders and racers gather after the racing finishes each evening. It's a great place to see hot roddities of all shapes and sizes.

BELOW: Dad's distracted while I am having fun in my mini '32 Ford coupe stroller. This example accurately duplicates the shape and style of the real thing.

BELOW: This side car bike racer certainly cuts a low profile when racing at the Bonneville salt, but the whole arrangement does look somewhat precarious.

BOTTOM: Old dodgem car with matching trailer is a regular at the NSRA Nationals and always grabs its share of attention.

RIGHT: Another tidy street rod tag-along trailer that allows the passengers to bring along lots more luggage for the trip. This one has been highly finished in the same style as its host vehicle, right down to the same style chrome wire wheels. The tow car is a '37 Ford coupe.

BELOW: Swoopy, chopped Chevy Aeromaster should naturally have a matching trailer with equally swoopy styling and this one suits perfectly. The teardrop has matching roofline sweep to the host vehicle and it's coated in matching bright red lustrous paint.

ABOVE: Ford delivery vans like this superbly finished '56 F100 panel are rare in their own right but this one has a unique drivetrain. Look in the engine bay of the bright yellow vehicle and you will find that the owner, Bill Nelson opted for an east-west mounted Cadillac Northstar engine and transmission.

ABOVE & RIGHT: Beautifully rebuilt and improved Buick convertible sedan exhibits class from end to end and appears to have a matching Buick engine. Look again – it's actually a big block Chevy engine dressed up to look like a Buick item – very cool!

ABOVE: Martina and Darren Hoffmann own this one of a kind "Li'l Tug Boat" '55 Chevy snub nose COE Cameo. Obviously made from a COE cabin, it's fitted with a Gibbs Racing 409 stroked to 473 and has Candy Root Beer paint with Tangerine highlights.

LEFT & RIGHT: We see so many fake Olds Rocket engines these days it is nice to come across the real thing as shown here in Marshall Woolery's '32 Ford coupe. At right is a typical fake version, actually a small block Chevy engine with aftermarket "Oldsmobile Rocket" rocker covers.

ABOVE: Why wouldn't you chop up an old fast-back Mustang to use as a trailer camper behind your street rod Model A Ford? "One half trick pony" started life as a '69 Mustang that now rides along behind on a pair of Cragar S/S wheels. Black and white photo indicates that this one was taken before the advent of digital cameras and full colour magazines, that makes it pre 2000 at least.

LEFT & BELOW: Back in 1974 VW made a vehicle called a Thing. That's a stock one shown below. The one at left has been "recommisioned" as a fairgrounds cruiser by owner Taylor Clark. It's been dropped, had the doors removed and the windshield folded and the passengers now sit on "park benches". What fun!

RIGHT: Tom and Jane Harris' green '40 Ford coupe might make you stop and stare because something looks different. Yes it is, the body and hood have been subtley sectioned to give the coupe a lower profile that isn't readily apparent. Adding to the deception is the use of a '39 Ford Deluxe grille, the door handles moved up into the body trim line and '41 Studebaker taillights fitted.

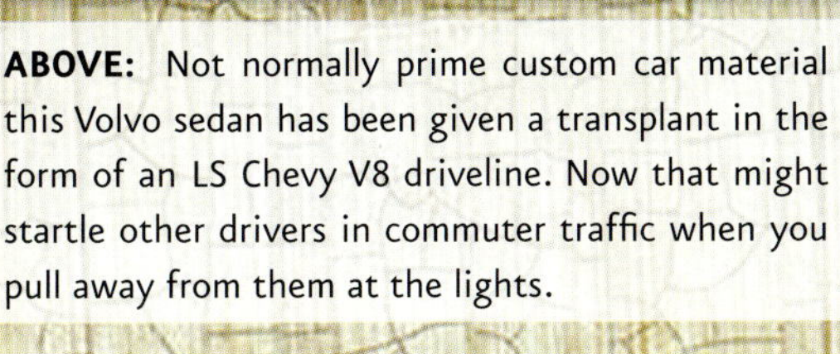

ABOVE: Not normally prime custom car material this Volvo sedan has been given a transplant in the form of an LS Chevy V8 driveline. Now that might startle other drivers in commuter traffic when you pull away from them at the lights.

LEFT: Roll into the Street Rod Nationals in a rodded Bentley and people will take notice. This superb example is owned by Kyle and Kathy Smith from Starcity Hot Rods in Trontville, VA.

BELOW LEFT: They will take just as much notice if you turn up in a contraption like the "T-Tanic". a humorous take on the boat-tail speedster theme that ventured to Bonneville. It uses an actual inverted boat as the rear of the body and a wooden boat steering wheel.

BELOW: There isn't much space for luggage in a '32 Ford Vicky so add some more by using a matching rod trailer like this one. Add a chrome plated carry rack for a nifty Coca-Cola ice box and you have the complete travelling outfit.

BELOW: Not a model that you see every day and even rarer as a customised cruiser is Bud Wolfe's sleek '60 Edsel that sits low to the ground and rolls on large diameter billet wheels. Edsels are often considered ugly, but there's nothing ugly about Bud's delightful example.

BELOW: Aussie utes make great street rods and they respond well to some mild custom work. This one owned by Mike and Diane Holmes has rounded corners at the rear of the ute bed and it has been fitted with sedan type rear fenders. Original rear fenders on this '37 model were a simpler, rounded shape. Note the recessed license plate and central single exhaust outlet too. Shiny wheels and nice gunmetal grey paint finish it off.

ABOVE: Getting around the Louisville fairgrounds in Kentucky can be quite a task for the not so able bodied, so why not do it in absolute comfort by using a racing seat on a custom built polished aluminum gofer. Adding a similar custom made trailer with its own padded seat means a friend can come along too.

ABOVE: Here's another rod with the mild custom body treatment to improve the squarish body lines, this time a '34 Dodge pickup owned by Denny Olsen. Dropping in a detailed 392 Hemi engine, leaving off the bumpers and adding shiny billet wheels works on this one too. Butcher Fabrications did the clean bodywork.

ABOVE: Theming a trailer to match the tow-car always adds an element of class as seen on this Deuce coupe combination. The trailer is a simple aftermarket commercial item but once painted to match the tow car and fitted with the same style wheels it all comes together.

LEFT: No, Chevy didn't make a '57 El Camino but that didn't stop this owner making one of his own that we snapped at the 2019 Tri-Five Chevy Nationals in Bowling Green, KY. Possibly made from a sedan or station wagon.

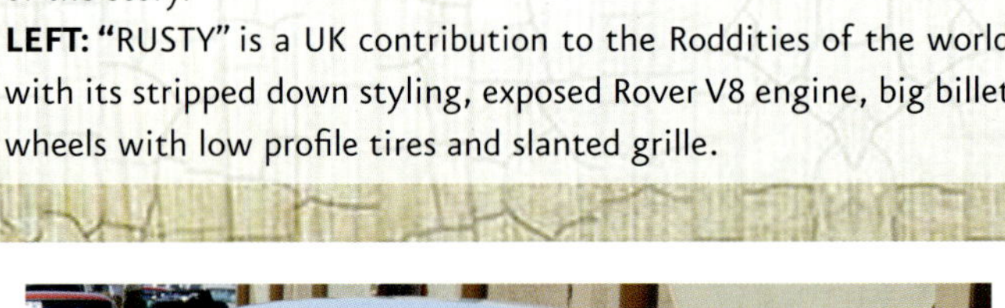

ABOVE: Now this is taking the tractor grille look to the extreme on a rat rod style pickup. The entire front half of a McCormick Farmall has been added instead of the more common grille section only.

ABOVE LEFT: Have some inexpensive cruising fun at the Summernats by taking an old EJ Holden sedan and cutting off the roof, adding some corrugated iron fender skirts and converting the trunk to a rumble seat. The plowshear windsplitter adds a nice finishing touch and the smiles on the passengers' faces tell the rest of the story.

LEFT: "RUSTY" is a UK contribution to the Roddities of the world with its stripped down styling, exposed Rover V8 engine, big billet wheels with low profile tires and slanted grille.

LEFT & ABOVE: Shock-horror, someone cut my Rolls Royce! Actually it was Jack from Castro Valley, California who reworked his '59 Rolls Royce by chopping the top and dropping it right down over the suspension to give the former luxo-cruiser a whole new slant on life. There's a big V8 in the engine bay too.

ABOVE: Here's a unique way to tour the fairgrounds once you park your Chevy, take the matching '57 Chevy bicycle and tour by foot pedal power.

ABOVE: Nothing like being prepared for any eventuality, but hopefully the twin caskets will remain a trailer for the foreseeable future.

ABOVE: Really cool ice chest is completely decked out to match the owner's '56 Chevy Nomad. How cool is that? A Nomad ice chest!

BELOW: Cool, cut-down VW Kombi camper makes a neat sleep out for Andrew Chaddock behind his Anglia.

ABOVE & LEFT: Leo Payne combined elements of '31 Ford coupe and sedan bodies to come up with a unique "phantom" body for his street rod. The flathead V8 powered "coupedan" is also mounted on a '32 Ford chassis and uses cowl mounted steering.

RIGHT: One more odd-ball trailer, this time a matching Anglia based unit done somewhat in town car delivery style with roadster style forward section and closed rear. The tow car wears a few changes too, note the extended front fenders and ribbed steel roof insert.

TOP LEFT: The Buff Express, a unique trailer that is a tribute to the owner's father, James E. Johnson who retired after 37 years with the US Post Office.

TOP RIGHT: Double your Nationals fun with a scooter and trailer seat that saves walking the long distances involved at the Louisville, KY fairgrounds.

ABOVE: No, there never was a three window '38 Ford coupe, this one was a five window converted to three by owner Woody Smith. There's a surprise under the hood too. Yes it's a flathead but this one is a V12 Lincoln version.

LEFT: No shame if you don't recognise this German built '39 Hanomag seen at the Euro Nats in the UK. Hanomag turned to military production for the war and never made cars again.

ABOVE: Steve Becker's Morris Minor Estate Wagon is a neat little rod with a great big heart in the form of a monstrous supercharged big block Chevy engine. I bet that would be an exciting ride at wide open throttle on the freeway! Steve had the black wagon on display at the 2019 NSRA Street Rod Nationals in Louisville, KY.

ABOVE, LEFT & BELOW: Larry Fuller from Benny Lake, WA owns this outstanding '35 International pickup with 392 Hemi running gear. Sharp-eyed readers will notice that it actually uses '34 Ford fenders and running boards and is fitted with a custom built pickup bed.

ABOVE: Someone dropped the boat on top of the car! Oh well, let's go to the Street Rod Nationals anyway, nobody will notice.

RIGHT: One more rod trailer with matching Coca-Cola ice box, all done in sparkling bright red paint with matching wheels to its host '36 Ford three window coupe.

BEACH HOP
ROCK 'N 'ROLL FESTIVAL

ABOVE: Lisa Sawyer's refreshing white hiboy 1930 Model A Ford coupe has been on a roll. It took out Top Car at both the Street Rod Nationals and Beach Hop. Lisa runs with Bay Rodders in Tauranga.

New Zealand

Words: Craig Stare
Photos: Craig Stare

Words: Craig Stare
Photos: Craig Stare

With COVID-19 hitting New Zealand in March only a couple of weeks before the scheduled event, decisions had to be made in a hurry. Noddy (the organiser) quickly made the right call to postpone the Beach Hop until November 25-29 of the same year. But would it work? Sure did!

As it was the 20 year anniversary all the merchandise had already arrived. A few entrants cancelled but their places were quickly snapped up by others. But the 20th anniversary needed to happen in 2020.

Entry numbers were still at 1500, so there was plenty to see. Tuesday night's weather was horrible, but Wednesday's run to Waihi was pretty good with only a few showers. Thursday was good day for the run to Whitianga, a beautiful coastal resort where the entrants completely took over the town. That night at Williamson Park saw a concert featuring Kiwi rock legends from the past.

The long awaited "Thundercruise" took place on the Friday, only a short drive from Whangamata to Onemana, but due to the strong contingent of cars the trip took almost 1-1/2 hours to complete!

Every night there was main street cruising, bands playing all over town and cars everywhere. Saturday was the grand parade and show day with various themed areas all over town. Every street you came to was filled to capacity with about another 1000 cars, not actually entered for the event.

By Sunday the giveaway car had been dealt with and the Nostalgia fair was in full swing, then the heavens opened up and the 20 year anniversary was all but over. No 21 will be back at its March time slot. ∎

ABOVE: Rare 1966 Mercury Colony Park is the ultimate beach cruiser, long roof and surfboards complete the picture.
LEFT: This T bucket was all business with blown small block Chevrolet and roll cage – and street legal too!

BELOW: This HQ Holden station wagon was a real "sleeper" that appeared to be powered by an injected big block Chevrolet engine.

LEFT: Kevin Satler's uncommon 1939 Ford standard coupe runs 351 Cleveland with four speed top loader manual transmission. Kevin is a member of East Bay Rods in Auckland and his coupe rols on Salt Lake Special wheels. The bright red coupe has been extensively decromed and runs bumperless, resulting in a clean overall appearance.

TOP LEFT: Brendan Armstrong's candy burgundy chopped 1933 Ford three window coupe sits perfect and is very slick.

TOP RIGHT: A bunch of young rodders "cruised the wheels off" this patina'd 1960 Ford Fairlane two door, powered by a blown 460 Ford.

ABOVE: Mike Wells from Whakatane keeps "churning out" these amazing vintage caravans, the detailing is beyond description.

ABOVE RIGHT: Dave Murtagh's Wellington based, pearl orange 1964 Ford Galaxie was Top Car in 2019 and it made the Top 5 again this year.

RIGHT: Clint Wheeler returned in 2020 with a new build. A perfect FJ Holden panel van, also making it to the Top 5 cars.

BELOW: A perfect place for a picnic. Hundreds of rods parked up at Friday's run to Onemana with hundreds more lining the cruise route.

TOP: The giveaway car, a perfect 1965 Ford Mustang convertible seen here been driven by Noddy, the man behind the organisation of Beach Hop each year.

ABOVE: Monaros are making a huge comeback this HQ model was a very classy build.

TOP: Neat steel '32 Ford five window coupe in black primer with dropped headlight bar is Ian Goodwins' latest toy.

ABOVE: This perfect 1971 Chevelle with a blown big block Chev engine comes in for some close inspection.

BELOW: Lowriders have always been a feature of the Beach Hop. Josh Trybula just finished this candy red 1963 Chev Impala convertible from Upper Hutt.

LEFT: Low riding, two tone 1957 Buick Special four door hardtop looks great with 20-inch diameter five spoke wheels. Crowds line the streets of Whangamata to watch the passing spectacle.

BELOW: A previous Australian show winning 1931 Model A Victoria with Deuce grille from Queensland is now owned by Suzy Mattock from Matamata.

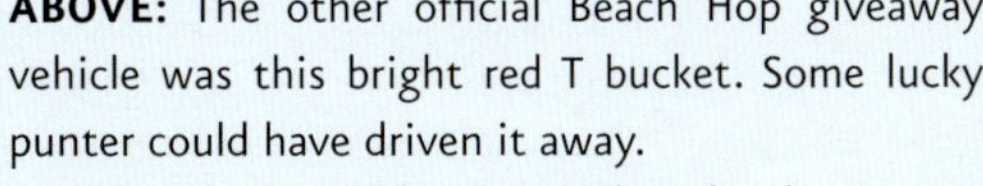

ABOVE: The other official Beach Hop giveaway vehicle was this bright red T bucket. Some lucky punter could have driven it away.

RIGHT: Who would have ever thought that a 1961 Ford Fairlane could look so good, slammed on the ground and fitted with chromies.

BELOW LEFT: Retro caravans were everywhere. Around 80 of them were on display, many had entrants living in them for the entire event.

BELOW RIGHT: An outrageous chopped 1947 Ford Jailbar "tip truck", all bathed in glossy black paint.

LEFT: Each night the main drag saw hundreds of cool cars cruising, including this 1959 Pontiac coupe that rides on steel wheels with baldy caps and trims.

BELOW: At first glance this 1948 Chev pickup looks fairly staunch, a closer inspection under the bonnet confirmed that by revealing a twin blown V10 Viper in the engine bay.

BELOW: "TETNIS", what could be a more appropriate rego plate for a rare, patina covered 1959 Mercury Commuter wagon? Love the hardtop roofline.

ABOVE: Prime spot for viewing the night cruising, Mum and the kids in the trunk of a HR Holden. That's much more fun than having a bedtime story!

RIGHT: Justin Walker's roof chopped 1964 Galaxie features a blown big block Ford and was top car at Beach Hop in 2018. Justin hails from New Plymouth.

ABOVE & INSET: Rocket Speed equipment spent many long hours finishing Brad Marsh's stunning candy blue big back window F100. The main shot shows it amongst the countless cars after Friday's Onemana Beach Cruise.

RIGHT: Tidy 1962 Ford Galaxie looked good with turquoise metallic paint and the simple addition of chromies and whitewalls.

ABOVE: A wild 1951 Ford pickup, this model is known as a "Bonus" model in New Zealand.

LEFT: Chopped 1934 Ford coupe "JUICD" uses orange pearl paint and American five spoke wheels to stand out from the crowd.

LEFT: Liz Gracie is the queen of the burnout pad but she enjoys driving her blown 1969 Camaro to hot rod events as well.

BELOW LEFT: There were a number of 1961 Chevrolet Impala bubble tops at the "Hop" and this was riding on American Racing wheels one of the cleanest around.

BELOW: Not only was there a nice XA Falcon coupe at this house but dad had built an exact replica so "junior" could participate in Beach Hop as well.

ABOVE LEFT: Two lovely ladies were seen quite often out cruising in this nicely improved green HQ Holden Monaro.

LEFT: Not entered for the event but spotted on a side street was this good looking, low 1961 Ford Starliner. Its elegant but simple styling looks perfect in bright red with polished wheels.

RIGHT: Another bubble top, this time in the form of a 1961 Buick Invicta. The colour, wheels and trim made this air ride equipped beauty one of my favourites.

BELOW: Joining the Top 5 group was Steve Milne's 1956 Chevrolet 210 two door sedan from Tauranga. Perfection in detail.

BELOW RIGHT: A very rare car in any country is this imported, restored 1937 Ford sedan delivery owned by Des Rider from Auckland.

ABOVE: Fully restored 1950 Pontiac two door sedan was refreshingly different, it even had a matching caravan.

ABOVE RIGHT: How long has it been since you have seen a perfect Anglia panel van, or is it a Thames?

RIGHT: Nice XA/XB Falcon coupes like this clean example are "Ozzy" classics that are steadily climbing in value. Note the custom door release and hidden wiper treatment on the engine hood.

Cool Hand Tommy

PROFILE: TOM EASTON – DRAG RACER

ABOVE: Wild wheelstand at Heathcote Park was successfully saved and the run completed, despite bending the front end. It convinced officials that Tommy really could drive! This was the first version of the altered that was named Super Screw – because Tommy was a carpenter!

BELOW: Tommy's last version of race car, the KB powered, Sidchrome sponsored altered that started out as the one above and evolved over time to one of the fastest altereds in the world.

Tommy Easton was born in Dimboola and moved around a bit from there until the family ended up in the Melbourne suburb of Hampton. It was a tough area in those days, but Tommy was alert, noticing that people from nearby Brighton were a little bit "toffy", but he recognised the benefit of buying into that area as the house values would appreciate. It was a move that would pay off for Tommy in later years.

"As a kid, Dad always made stuff that got us out of, or into trouble. I was into push-bikes, picking up bits from the tips and making them into something we could use. I always had a fast billycart, and about the age of 16, started playing around with cars – learning to drive in a paddock bomb Morris 10 that had no brakes. I learnt to control it – a move that played out in the future, as I had no fear of fast cars or dicey racing situations."

Building that confidence in his own driving ability paid dividends later when Tommy started drag racing – a clutch failure in his HD Holden at 110 mph left him with no brakes but he managed to steer the car into a dam at end of Calder Raceway and he escaped unharmed. Not so the HD!

"My first street car was an FC Holden, when most young guys were into FJs, FCs etc. This car was purchased from

ABOVE LEFT: The FJ was Tommy's first car that he drag raced. Coolness personified!
LEFT & ABOVE: Tom's HD Holden was a bright performer that came to grief at Calder when a clutch failed at high speed. He still has the original rego plate.

locally in Hampton, where it was rebuilt by Kenny Hurrie. It had a rolled pan, good grey motor and could even give GT Falcons a run. Unfortunately it was T-boned by an old dear and that destroyed the car. The FC was replaced by an FJ into which I put a 186S and four speed with Wade cam, Yella-Terra head, triple SUs, eight inch wheels with street race tyres and that one did embarrass a lot of GTs, it was as quick as a 750 Honda.

The FJ was followed by the 327 powered HD Holden from Max Kirwan Motors that I bought with the V8 already installed with a four speed transmission and pipes that ran through the inner guards. Even though it was a stock motor, I drove it like a race car, consequently revved it too hard and blew it up. I used to read the American magazines and books like Car Craft etc., where I read a story by the Chevy engineer Smokey Yunick – the top performance man in those days. In particular there was an article on how to get 450 HP with a "Smokey" manifold. Use of a flat tappet off-road factory cam meant this combination was a real mongrel, it did nothing under 3000 rpm, but really came to life from there. It was fitted with 2.02 fuellie heads that were ported by John English, the internals were balanced and it ran 12:1 compression – a real animal.

At Calder it ran 13.0 at 115 mph on Bridgestone tyres which was very good performance for those days. I destroyed the car when the clutch pressure plate exploded near the finish line at Calder, cutting through the floor, brake lines etc., and a piece of the clutch even hit the timing tower right on an upright – there was a guy standing directly behind it! The HD went through the finish line, off the track and out into the paddocks, finally hitting a dam that had formed from recent rain and it stopped in the water. The wild ride distorted the car so badly that the doors wouldn't open, it was buggered!"

www.graffitipub.com.au

TOP B&W: Running against Ian Splatt at Heathcote Park Raceway many years ago. Tommy also spent a short time on Rachelle Splatt's Top Fuel team. **CLOCKWISE FROM ABOVE:** Old sign reading "Tom Easton Drive" hung on the fence at Calder Raceway. Ready for a run at Calder in the "Super Screw" altered. Trying Glen Davis' land speed car for size – he didn't fit! Tommy stepped into go-karts for a while and was immediately competitive. The crutches were from a non-race incurred injury and he went ahead and drove the altered despite the doctor recommending against it.

OPPOSITE PAGE: More of Tommy's project cars (see text) and a photo from a trouble-shooting exercise in the Calder pits on The Pirotta Cortina. The HD Holden is the one that suffered a clutch explosion at Calder, resulting in the running gear being transferred to the HR van, while the customised Bedford van had a mid-mounted 400 Chevy engine with four wheel disc brakes controlled by a Mazda master cylinder/booster combination. Tommy's first major crash at Heathcote Park Raceway following an engine explosion that oiled the slicks. He was still doing 176 mph when the car hit the fence.

LEFT: The Cobra is based on an RCM kit that Tom acquired about 1990 but it sat for 10 years before work commenced in earnest. It is powered by a stroked 347 Windsor with Edelbrock alloy heads that is fed by eight throttle body injection controlled by an Autronic computer. Transmission is four speed BTR automatic and the rear end is a narrowed item from an XJ6 Jaguar. Wheels are 10x18 and 8x18 BMW M5 Motorsport fitted with Mickey Thompson street radials. Paintwork is Black Cherry candy and the interior trim is black leather. A carbon fibre dash holds VDO gauges while the steering wheel is a Grant with leather wrap. The lift-off hard top roof was designed and made by Tom.

ABOVE & BELOW: Tom acquired this blown small block Chevy powered hiboy Model A roadster on '32 rails as part payment for the race car when he retired from racing. He only kept the roadster for a short time and then sold it to reduce debt.

Tommy then bought a HR panel van and transferred the running gear from the HD into it and continued racing.

"Then I started to get interested in genuine competition cars. I raced against a Chevy Nova that was a full-on race car and beat it – the guy was fuming, 'Beaten by a street car!' In the early '80s I bought a race car from Murray Anderson; the chassis had been built at Dragway, welded by Brian Ball who died from cancer. Murray Anderson fitted a T bucket body to the chassis. At the time Ian Splatt was really well known from building and driving the Bounty Hunter altered with big block Chevy engine. My car was set up with a small block and fuel injection and gradually evolved into the monster it became. I picked up lots of knowledge along the way, but I was helped a lot by Adrian Ghirenghelli and Peter Russo (and his great family). Peter had bad eyesight and tended to drive by ear, which was very entertaining.

I ran the small block for a few seasons. Adrian had a very quick altered and I started to get close to him and another top racer from Adelaide. Then I decided to go big block and add a blower after I had unsuccessfully tried a blower on the small block. By going to the big block and fitted big iron heads, the car soon became the quickest and fastest BB altered in

ABOVE & BELOW: The yellow Torana started life as a standard sedan for which Tommy built a healthy 308 Holden V8 equipped with Yella Terra alloy heads and roller rockers. On top was an Edelbrock Torker manifold with Quadrajet carburettor and the engine was also fitted with a good ignition system and headers. Transmission was a Turbo 350 that came with the car as did the Simmonds wheels. Tommy fitted a complete SLR interior to make it look like a true SLR model and enjoyed driving it for a while. It was sold to help fund his Chevy Nova project.

Australia. That claim of quickest and fastest iron engine racer in the country, possibly still stands today."

When Tommy first built the race car he was working at pubs for extra money so that he could afford to go racing, sometimes working at three jobs at once.

"I didn't know what to call the car but, being a chippy, I decided to call it Super Screw – ANDRA didn't like it and said it was inappropriate – I sent a letter back telling them to get their heads out of the gutter, I'm a carpenter and I screw things together." They accepted it. The altered became a threat to the big hitters and I soon won a couple of races. Steve Brown

was putting together a full race team, which was unheard of in those days. He owned the Croydon Market and had a Nitro Funny Car – that was often driven by Graeme Cowin and Carter, sometimes even by visiting Americans. In 1986 he got Ray Ward and Wayne Rowe into the game. Then he asked me to join with my big block Altered. At the time I took a shine to the promo girl who is now my wife, Ana."

The car evolved into a very fast race car with 480 cube big block, but parts were too hard to find, so Tommy lashed out for a KB and it promptly became one of the fastest altereds in the world; fifth in the world actually, and second fastest in

Handy hire
trailers
055-343
347 c.i.
STROKER

Australia after Jeff Burnett who was the fastest. The best Tom ever achieved was to run 6.0 @ 220 mph.

"I was a bit of a favourite with the crowds because of the fearless driving – people thought I was crazy – I thought I was a good driver! The altered was always exciting to watch, a result of all that I learnt in the early days from playing with billycarts and pushbikes. I was never aggressive, but could always get the best out of my vehicles, no matter what. I never had accidents in the billycarts or on the bikes. When I graduated to cars we used to practise in wet weather to see who could do manoeuvres without hitting the curb. I never got out of control and never did hit the gutter. Later I took on go-karts when I was 48 years old and was immediately fast, in a fairly good water-cooled model with Rotax motor, sticky tyres etc. I was smooth, didn't wrestle with the steering wheel because if you did you were doing the wrong thing.

In the altered I pulled a monster wheelstand at Heathcote in late 1984, suddenly I was looking at sky and thought, 'Better crack the throttle to stop it flipping over.' Halfway down I hit the throttle again, but it still hit the strip fairly hard. I glanced at the gauges that all seemed okay, but I was on the throttle, so I stayed in it. When I got out at the end of the run the front end was dragging on the ground. Officials were always a bit toey when I ran but after that incident they came to recognise that I could drive. So-called experts couldn't believe I didn't get out of the throttle – in fact I did momentarily – but they didn't pick up on that. I always felt I was in control."

There were only two bad hiccups in Tommy's driving career, one at Heathcote and one at Sandown. At Heathcote the car suffered a blown engine that split the block and sprayed oil over the slicks and his helmet, so he couldn't see where he was going. The car went through the shut down area, Tommy thought he had it under control and popped the chute first, but all off a sudden it hit the left hand wall and it was still doing 176 mph!

ABOVE & RIGHT: Tom's latest project is this tidy '63 Chevy Nova that he purchased from the original importer in 2013. It was in poor condition but relatively rust-free and didn't have any accident damage, although the roof panel was badly pushed in. The Cyan Blue beauty now features Heidt's front suspension and an LSD 10 bolt rear end on single mono-leaf springs, plus a 383 small block Chevy engine fitted with AFR heads, an Edelbrock AVS2 intake and MSD ignition. Transmission is Turbo 700 with a B&M shifter. The interior uses VE Commodore ute seats but otherwise has the standard S/S trimmings with accessory gauges under the dash and a Grant steering wheel. Cal-Track tyres on 7x15 and 8x15 Convo Pro wheels add the finishing touch.

"That episode nearly broke me, so I ummed-and-ahhed about a rebuild but eventually decided to go ahead".

The next big crash was when doing a burnout demo at a Sandown truck show. The first burnout was a big success with a nice drift at the end but Tommy held it together just fine. The second burnout was later in the day after the Bandag Bullet truck had been doing circles and donuts that left a lot of tyre marks and rubber marbles on the surface of the track.

"As soon as I hit the marbles the car spun, hooked up sideways on the tyre marks and then barrel rolled four times. The impact knocked me out for a few minutes. Ana saw the car shake and that was the telltale to what happened. I stood up and waved to the crowd, but it put me out of racing for a few years. This was at the same time, April 1994, when Senna and Ratzenberger were killed in their Formula 1 race cars."

The next year, Ian Splatt approached Tommy to crew on Rachelle's top fueller.

"Splatty asked me who built good engines? The answer was, 'I do – everything else too, transmissions, rear ends etc.' I was on the team for a couple of race meetings, but didn't get on with the crew chief (a Canadian). He tried to tell me what to do, but I told him I knew what I was doing. Well that didn't work, so it didn't last. The next season I got my own car back on the track and went faster and faster until I finally reached that 6.0 @220 mph pass at the Nationals in 2000."

In the later years Tommy had VDO sponsorship – all done on a handshake deal. Then Sidchrome offered him a contract, so they became the major sponsors. New people took over and Calder shut down, so that meant he couldn't fulfil the number of events they required, so Sidchrome tore up the contract.

"That was it for my racing days, but I couldn't stay away from cars so I got into a Model A hiboy hot rod on '32 rails with a blown 350, low cut windscreen and roof that I accepted as part payment for the race car. It was followed by the Cobra and Chevy Nova that I own now. I gave the hot rod a workout one day by stomping on the throttle and it promptly turned left, so I got out of it because it didn't handle very well. Ultimately I had to sell it to reduce debt early in 2000. It went for $65,000.00 – good money for those days. The race car went to Walfords in Sydney in ready-to-race condition."

A good friend of Tommy's got involved in HQ racing. He was a panel beater and asked Tom to build him an engine. For this class of racing all engines had to run a specified cam etc., the only thing to do was get as much compression into the engine as possible, retard the camshaft and put in a real good ignition. Richard Fairlam, the owner, competed in his first event at Sandown where he was creaming them all, pulling away from the field. They all got up in arms, reckoned he was cheating, so they had to tear the engine down to reveal nothing out of the ordinary, it was just put together properly. Ana worked for Glenn Seton, who got Tommy involved in go-karts where he won the first event he competed in – the over 40s class. That rattled a few cages too.

Since ending his competitive race days Tommy has concentrated on his and Ana's 60 acre property and he spends his time building engines for hot rodder friends. Like driving, engine building always came easy to Tommy Easton.

BELOW: Tommy's trophy cabinet would be the envy of any drag racer. It takes pride of place in his home based workshop where he now builds engines for his hot rodder friends.

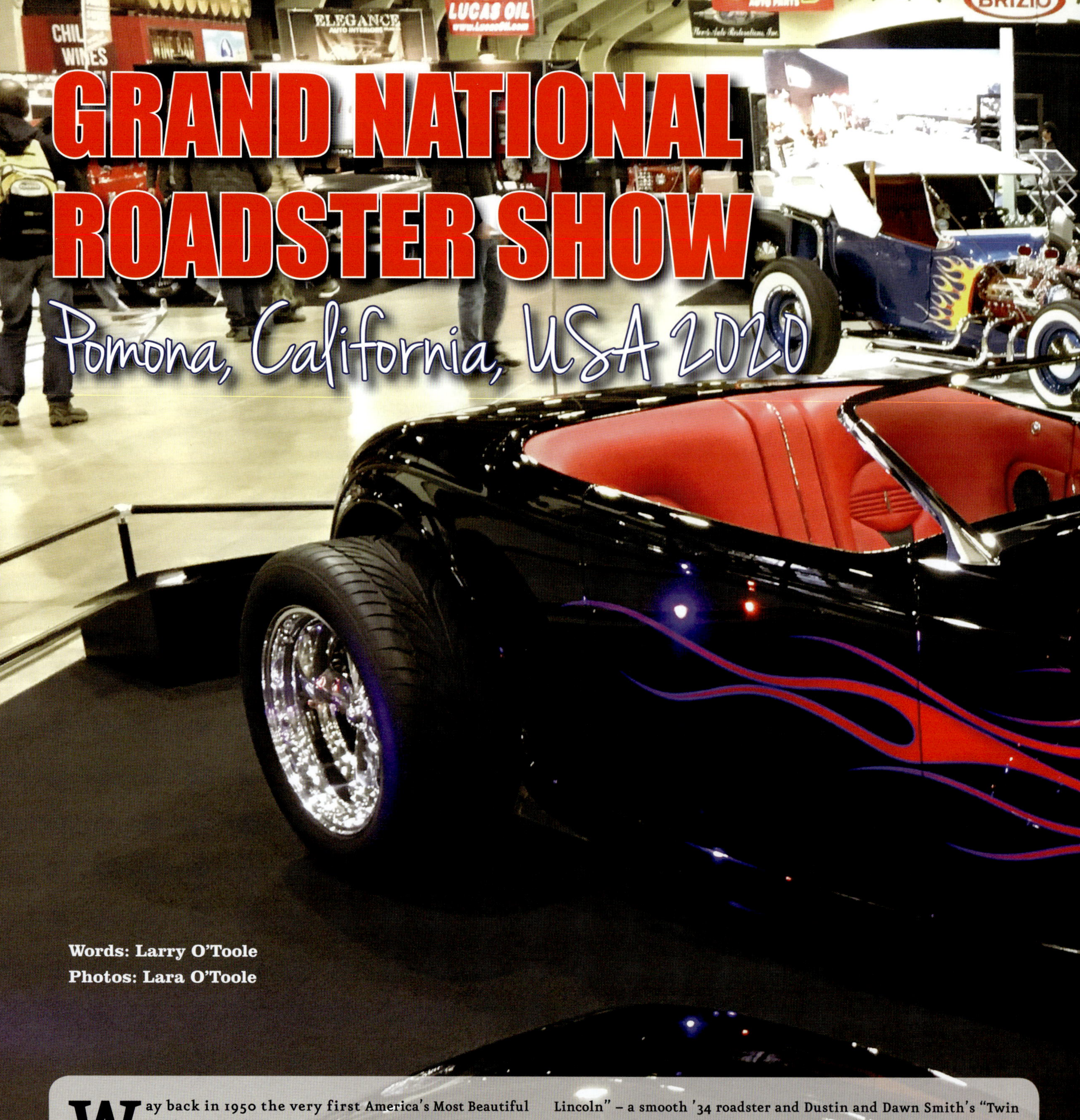

GRAND NATIONAL ROADSTER SHOW
Pomona, California, USA 2020

Words: Larry O'Toole
Photos: Lara O'Toole

Way back in 1950 the very first America's Most Beautiful Roadster award was made and seventy years later Monty Bellsham has joined the long list of impressive winners. Included in that list are such famous names as George Barris in 1962 and LeRoi "Tex" Smith in 1963 - both with 1927 Ford roadsters, Andy Brizio in 1970 with a 1923 Ford roadster pickup and Boyd Coddington in 1996 with his '32 Ford roadster.

Monty's winning '32 Ford roadster was among a field of 10 immaculate cars vying for the prestigious award on this occasion, his competition including a stunning red '32 Ford roadster from Japan presented in memory of its owner, Ken Katashio who passed away whilst building it, the sparkling "Leg Show T" 1915 Model T Bucket owned by Walter Sigsbey of Los Angeles, Brandie Laird's "Lady Laird

Lincoln" – a smooth '34 roadster and Dustin and Dawn Smith's "Twin Fan Special", a '27 T Ford roadster from Washington state.

The GNRS paid homage to drag racing with an entire pavilion dedicated to its "Drag Racing Then and Now" display featuring funny cars, pro stocks, fuel altereds, super gassers, junior dragsters and top fuellers, including that of the "First Lady of Drag Racing", Shirley Muldowney. The display had a heavy representation of those that hit strips across Southern California in the early-to-mid '60s with some built as early as 1958.

The 2020 Grand National Roadster Show also opened its arms to an outdoor display of more than 500 pre-1973 hot rods, customs, classics, muscle cars and trucks for the 16th Annual Grand Daddy Drive-In in the Fairplex grounds over the weekend.

ABOVE: Monty Bellsham presented his Kugel Muroc Roadster no 4, one of 10 built by Kugel, this one originally for Nick Barron. Monty wanted to make it look more like a hot rod so he purchased it and had Squeeg's Kustoms give the car a revamp. The roadster is powered by a Hilborn injected LS 1 Chevy engine. The outstanding roadster was the America's Most Beautiful Roadster winner for 2020.

ABOVE: "Aquaman" is Jerry Logan's 1957 Ford Fairlane 500 that was built by Richard Zocchi. It features a chopped top, nosed, decked and shaved body, custom taillights, tubular grille and custom mixed PPG Aqua paint with fogged body accents. The modified original chassis has full air-ride suspension, 351 Windsor engine with Holley carb and rolls on chrome reversed wheels with cone centre caps and wide whitewall tyres.

ABOVE: From Santa Maria, CA was Jerry and Lorrie Jacobs' 1957 Chevy Belair. Paint is candy Brandywine, trim is candy charcoal and the top has been sectioned 2-1/2 inches. The body has also been shaved and the vent windows removed. Chassis Works did the chassis and added a 12 point roll cage.

BELOW: John and Sonia Breslow's '32 Ford Vicky sits just right on chrome wire wheels and was turned out by the folks at Team Brizio.

ABOVE LEFT: Wild Willys convertible is a 1941 model that obviously features air-bag suspension and big billet wheels, plus a custom made alligator style hood.

ABOVE: The Grand National Roadster how is a big event with lots of different classes and sections so there is a correspondingly large array of trophies to be taken home at the end of the show.

LEFT: Hard to beat the simple styling of this hiboy Deuce five window coupe with red painted steel wheels, trim rings and caps with a pair of Guide headlights leading the way up front.

GNRS 2020

ABOVE: Designed by Thom Taylor in 1989 and built by Boyd Coddington in 1990, this yellow '32 Ford three window coupe has recently been restored by Team Brizio for Bill and Lyn Currie of Harvard, MA.

ABOVE RIGHT: House of the Rising Sun displayed their custom painting skills on the House of Kolor stand.

RIGHT: Bob Pierson's 1936 Competition Coupe appeared on the cover of Hot Rod Magazine way back in August 1948!

BELOW: Check out the outlandish custom paint scheme on Dana Hinkle's, 1930 Ford Tudor. It was entered in the Altered Street Sedan class.

LEFT: Mike Dwight from Gilroy, CA owns this 1932 Ford Roadster "Lil Evil". Running gear consists of a 347 cubic inch small block Ford with Tremec five speed manual transmission and a Winters quick-change rear end. Mel Green, Jack Hageman Jr, Roy Brizio and John Leonti get special mention for their work on the project.

BELOW: Gary and Deborah Devine's '32 Ford "War Paint" was built by Denny Lesky from Inonia Hot Rod Shop and Dave Shuten from Galpin Speed Shop. Hot Dog laid on the PPG Envirobase paintwork and the interior trim is by Elegance Auto Interiors.

ABOVE & INSET: The famous "Leg Show" T bucket is based on a 1915 Ford and is owned by Walter and Thenia Sigsbey. The wild creation features Wilwood brakes, Dank Fink grille and paint by Dan Gogh.

GNRS 2020

LEFT: "Just a big ol' Fiascoe" is the '47 Ford COE of Jeff and Jaime Chambers. Tucked underneath is Accuair E-Level suspension, a 383 Stroker engine with Holley Sniper fuel injection, 700R4 transmission and there's Vintage Air inside for passenger comfort. Standley Bros Hot Rods were the builders of this PPG Fiascoa Green beauty.

BELOW LEFT: The Original Kookie Kar '22 T bucket is now owned by Ross and Beth Myers from Boyertown, PA. It was restored by Roy Brizio Street Rods with body and paint by Vintage Colour Studio.

BELOW: "The Mower Roadster" is a '32 Ford that has Chevrolet LS-1 engine and belongs to Gary Mower from Big River, CA.

ABOVE & INSET: "K's Roadster" is a fully fendered '32 Ford owned by Len Latashio from Yokohama, Japan. It features Deuce Factory chassis, Rod Bods all steel body, GM fast burn 383 ci 425hp engine, Richamond five speed transmission, Halibrand quick-change rear end and PS Engineering Kidney Bean wheels with Firestone tyres. The Boyd Red Colour was sprayed by Andys Rod Works.

RIGHT: If you aren't a fan of showy hot rods, Ben Weatherbee's bare metal '31 Ford Coupe with Buick Nailhead engine should be more to your liking. It was displayed in the "Suede Palace" section.

LEFT: Jeremy Jack's '31 Model A Ford Pickup was displayed it in the Suede Palace section. The flathead powered pickup rides on a Deuce chassis and sports a Deuce grille up front.
BELOW: The Twin Fan Special is Dustin and Dawn Smith's original steel bodied '27 T roadster pickup that features an uncommon flathead Ford six cylinder engine.

BELOW: David Perry owns this Australian '35 Ford roadster ute. It's an original Ford ute body with two inch top chop, Chevy 383, Turbo-Hydro 350 transmission and nine inch Ford rear end that was owner-built and painted.

BELOW: Stefan Immke of Fallbrook, CA entered his '32 Ford Roadster that was built by Nostalgia Ranch. It uses a fully dressed flathead, '39 Ford three speed manual transmission and Halibrand rear end.

ABOVE: "The Browstone Roadster" belongs to Tom Firth and Jodi Lant and was built by Stokers Hot Rod Factory. The '32 Ford is painted Brownstone Metallic with leather interior trim by Elegance of Upland.

ABOVE: From the Impala Palace came this '63 Chevy "Impalamino" custom phantom pickup based on a '63 full size Chevy that was entered by Aaron Long from Alamo, CA. It is so well executed that it looks factory!

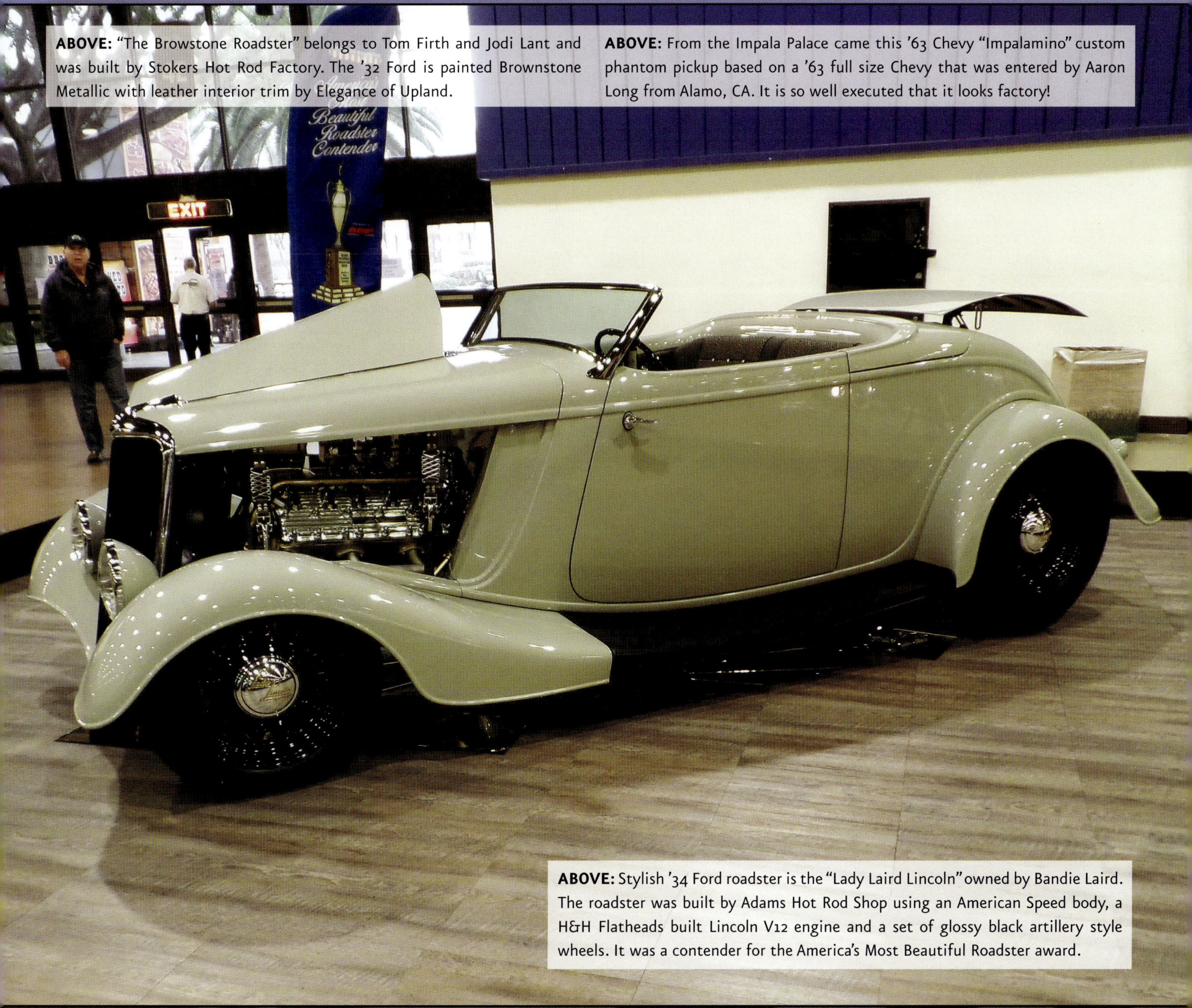

ABOVE: Stylish '34 Ford roadster is the "Lady Laird Lincoln" owned by Bandie Laird. The roadster was built by Adams Hot Rod Shop using an American Speed body, a H&H Flatheads built Lincoln V12 engine and a set of glossy black artillery style wheels. It was a contender for the America's Most Beautiful Roadster award.

LEFT & BELOW LEFT: "Malachite" is the '60 Cadillac Coupe DeVille owned by Joe and Angela Wallem that has been treated to an extensive custom paint scheme in two shades of green over a white background.

BELOW: Whitewalls on chrome wheels with '50 Mercury hub caps set the tone for this mildly chopped '28 Model A Ford Tudor with Deuce grille, flathead running gear, white top material and matching white interior trim.

MAIN PIC: John Ivy, had a short trip from nearby Azusa, CA to enter his outstanding '27 Model T Ford Roadster. Features include a well-executed track nose and fully dressed flathead engine.

LEFT: In the outside show area was this very tidy Deuce hiboy roadster with black cloth top, hood bulges, low mounted headlights and polished billet alloy wheels.

ABOVE: "Travellin" Blues" is a '54 Chevrolet 210 Kustom that belongs to Steven Scmidt from Fontana, CA.
LEFT: Club Pick went to Robert Rojas of, Hesperia CA for his 1954 custom Chevy 210 sedan finished in metalflake red.
BELOW: Cesar Lerma's flat black and blue '55 Oldsmobile Hardtop.

ABOVE: Now in the Petersen Museum Collection, the "0032" Roadster by Chip Foose won the AMBR award in 1996 when yellow and again in this black rendition in 2000.

ABOVE LEFT: George Poteet's superb '36 Ford roadster was back after winning the AMBR award in 2019.
ABOVE: The Barris-Seaton pearl white '55 Chevy Belair was built at Barris Kustoms in the period 1957-1958. It's 283 Chevy powered.

GNRS 2020

ABOVE: Nothing quite stirs the heart like a pair of front engine top fuel dragsters.

ABOVE: Bob and Derrick Jones' '32 Ford Tudor from Oregon is 396 Chevy powered with Turbo 400 auto, nine inch Ford rear end and vintage magnesium wheels.

ABOVE: Jake Steele's gasser style '40 Willys pickup.

MAIN PIC: Vintage altered drag car is a '27 T Ford Roadster owned by John Ivy of Azusa, CA. That's an injected small block Chevy providing the motive power.

ABOVE: Waynesville, OH is home for the '41 Willys Americar Coupe of Kevin Svarda. The all steel Willys won Best Engineered at the 1964 NHRA Nats.
BELOW: Another neat old front engine dragster, this one built in 1968 and owned by John Lipori of Marina, CA.

ABOVE: "The BBB Dragster" Dragster of Bob Smith was 1962 Winter Nationals Class Champion. Built in 1958 by Lefty Mutersbaugh, it uses a 301 ci Chevy, with Enderle Injection and Halibrand quick-change rear end.

RIGHT: The famous "Orange Crate" '32 Ford Sedan is now owned by Steven Gilligan from Vancouver, WA.

ABOVE: Early drag cars with the amazing four nailhead engine equipped '61 Buick "wagon" that was campaigned by TV Tommy Ivo and now owned by of Fred Engelhart, Rushford, MN in the foreground.

PICKIN'S

Pat Ganahl has been involved in the world of hot rodding publishing for most of his adult life. Now retired, Pat publishes a regular blog online (every other week) to keep himself and his many followers entertained. "PICKIN'S" is just one of these fascinating blogs, reproduced here in its entirety with Pat's permission.

My plan, given that I am held captive here at home during this time of COVID-19, same as you, was to take the time to rummage through my photo files, looking for interesting, unusual, or just plain cool images that haven't been seen before. Well.... I spent more than five full days, starting with one shoe-box of envelopes containing early color transparencies and some B&W negs, going back to the days before Rod & Custom was bought by Petersen. There were hundreds of photos just in that box. All good ones. Then I selected one binder (from a shelf of 25) marked "Early Color, Rods" which contained several hundred more images in clear sleeves. Again, all good, otherwise they wouldn't be there. I only got about halfway through that. So early yesterday I went out to the garage where I have two 5-drawer file cabinets filled with hanging files containing mostly B&W prints and proof sheets with negatives on the back. I started with a file labeled "Bill Burke Negs." These are what essentially started my collection, back in the mid-'70s. He gave me a whole box full of loose photos and negatives,

stating "You have more interest in history than I do." These photos go back to the early '30s (remember the SCTA was founded in late '37, and he was one of the founders). Then I tried files tagged Early Lakes and Early Rods. These were mostly 35mm proof sheets (36 images each) of photos from various old-timers' scrapbooks that I copied with my camera, years ago. Finally, pretty frustrated, I grabbed a file marked "Misc. Negs" this morning, and found three or four things I know you haven't seen.

But there are gobs more. More than I could begin to describe, let alone look through. My plan was to limit it to 25 photos. So. So... what follows certainly isn't "Best Of", or comprehensive, nor makes rhyme or reason. It's just a collection of "Pickin's". Hopefully something that will interest and entertain you during this time of COVID-19 internment.

There won't be much rhyme or reason to the order or time frame of photos here, either.

Hope you enjoy the "Pickin's".

LEFT: OK, let's jump way back in time. Wes Cooper's excellent track-nose '27 T roadster was featured on the cover of the Sept. '49 Hot Rod, with a two-page feature inside including a rare profile Rex Burnett cutaway drawing. Like the Spalding Bros. and Navarro roadsters, it featured the distinctive Art Ingles nose and grille, as well as his hood and bellypans. It had a Model B four-cylinder with a Fargo overhead, running four carbs and eight (doubled) connecting rods, good for an impressive 143+ mph at El Mirage. I've got plenty of photos if you want to see more, but only one like this.

LEFT & BELOW: I start with this one because I showed a tighter-cropped version, similar to the June '67 Car Craft cover, in my Instagram recently, and people wanted to know who took it and how. It was taken by the late Fred Enke, a busy and talented freelancer of the time. It was an annual L.A. Roadsters/Bay Area Roadsters meet, and I have an envelope with dozens of color photos. I like the one with waving car owners (see cover), but from this never-seen angle, Enke's shadow gives you a clue how he did it. Here you can see that it was a pretty elaborate set-up involving a hefty crane truck. I can't imagine doing this on the freelance pay I used to get! The envelope also contained many photos of the trip up to Sequoia Park, so I would assume that this parking lot was somewhere in the Visalia area, though I don't recognize the Carnation dairy background.

LEFT: The Jackman brothers' '32 Ford Sport Coupe from San Diego was a tour de force show car. This thing had a complete chromed frame, not to mention driveline, plus a Plexiglas floor to show it off, including 8 straight pipes that ran from the dual-quad T-Bird Y-Block to the back bumper. Even the license plates were chromed. I tried reducing the pink in this old 4×5 film, but that killed the brilliant hue of the candy wild cherry paint. This car was obviously selected as one of the top 75 Best Deuces for the 75th Anniversary bash at the Pomona Roadster Show. But with the original seemingly lost, Harry Jackman decided to build an exact clone, the painting of which I fully covered in my Custom Painting book. With the fresh candy wild cherry barely dry, and the clone positioned on the show floor, guess what rolled in next to it? Yes, the original Sport Coupe, out of nowhere (actually Colorado, I think), surprising everyone. The only major changes were black paint (with liberal white pinstriping) and a chopped top. I'm pretty sure I've got a photo of this, somewhere, if I can find it.

LEFT: You'll have to excuse the pink cast of this old Ektachrome. I've actually corrected this some, but I don't have Photoshop (nor time—or inclination—to mess with it). The car is painter/customizer George Cerney's '50 Olds, but as the window decal attests, Lyon's has installed a new '53 dual-quad Cad engine (as they did in Hirohata's Merc), punched to 377 inches and liberally chromed. While the car appears to be in primer, the whole engine compartment (including wires, cables, hinges, radiator) was sprayed luscious purple before the engine and chrome goodies were added.

RIGHT: It's hard to tell from this aged '54 photo whether Dave Bugarin's Barris '51 Merc is dark blue or purple (it was sapphire blue and metallic gray). You seldom see color photos of it, and definitely not from this rear angle, which I really like, with the (brand new) '54 Packard taillights frenched into the mildly extended '51 fenders. This one's apparently lost, though rumors persist that it's hidden somewhere in San Pedro.

ABOVE: You should recognize this as the Tony LaMasa roadster. But this photo was taken in Tony's Eagle Rock neighborhood in '51 (according to license plates) shortly after he got it. It looks like it's already painted metallic green. The bubble in the hood has a scoop cut in it. But it still has the three-carb flathead engine, and no Von Dutch striping. I like the way the cycle fenders were originally angled. I have an envelope of photos on this one, too, ostensibly taken for the new Rod & Custom little mag, (though it didn't appear until '53).

BELOW: Joe Bailon's style was way different from the Barris's—or anybody else's. And we're jumping ahead to 1959 to show Jim Doyle's, um, distinctive candy red '52 Merc convertible. To see how this car was found in deplorable condition on a Sacramento river levee, then restored, check my Lost Hot Rods II book. But the main reason I'm showing this photo here is because of the setting, with mid-century-modern motel, palms, sculpture(?), and full wall-art. The car just completes the concept.

ABOVE: This one hasn't turned pink, but it has faded a bit. It came from the shoebox full of envelopes, most of which were "outtakes" (i.e. leftovers) from freelance submissions to various magazines. But each envelope only had the name of the owner, type of car, and usually the photographer's name on it. All the information on this one was, "John Detrick, '51 Chevy Bel Air." It only had this one 2-1/4 x 2-1/4 transparency in it. It appears to be photographed on a golf course in the Glendale-Burbank area. Otherwise it was a complete mystery to me. But a quick Google search turned up one black and white image of the Chev (I would have guessed it was an Olds), with the name John Dietrich and "Valley Custom". Now remember I'm retired, and I shouldn't be doing research, but a little more digging turned up a HAMB entry on it from a few years ago, which in turn led me to a '55 Car Craft two page black and white feature (an issue missing from my incomplete collection). But nothing on the '40 coupe, which looks like it might be a little earlier (given the split '40-Lincoln bumpers), and looks really nice the closer you look (shaved and peaked hood, partially filled grille, shortened side chrome, white upholstery – and white spider painted on the cowl). Did the girl drive it there? Was it hers? But speaking of looking closer, that unassuming lady is very definitely flipping the bird with her left hand. Wow. Some photo. I guarantee you've never seen this one before. Then I got an email from my long-time Seattle pen-pal Bob Morrow stating that not only did Hot Rod do a one-page feature on the '40 in April '56, but he still has the page tacked to the back wall of his garage. The big surprise is that it ran a healthy chromed dual-quad Cad engine and what look like '41 Stude taillights. He also I.D.ed the finger-flipping girl as "starlet" Barbara Darrow. Look her up on Wikipedia to learn several surprising facts. Since the cars and Valley Custom were from the Glendale-Burbank area, I asked several local old-timers, including Alex Xydias, if they knew of either car or of Dietrich – nada, zip. Where are they?

LEFT: I've loved Sheldon Schmidt's blown Hemi '34 Comp Coupe since I first saw it in Hot Rod in '62. The candy tangerine is brighter than it looks here, but the tinted windows, chromed and detailed set-back engine, '34 grille, Moon tank, and polished 12-spokes add up to one bitchin-but-bad race car. Or show car? I've got a bunch of good photos of it, and one detail – a '39 Ford transmission inside – didn't equate. That blown Hemi would blow that trans in one or two runs. I remember I featured it in one of my books, and somehow I contacted Sheldon, who told me, "Yeah, that was just so I could get it in a magazine to get a sponsor." Which he did, and ran the car hard enough that he eventually catapulted off the end of the Pomona track (chute failure), across the road, landing upside down in the golf course on the other side. Not on fire, but still strapped in the seat, and bleeding. The safety crew saved him, but the car was lost.

BELOW: I also stated that Bill's photos went back into the mid-to-early '30s, as do others I was able to find and copy from other lakes veterans years ago. This one is obviously from the '30s at Muroc. The severely narrowed and bobbed (note gas tank at back) '27 T body makes it a "Modified." My notes state only that it has a Cragar head (presumably on a model B four) and a Hallock dual-carb intake. The dual-front-spring frame could be Essex, the narrow grille is from a Whippet, and it has shiny black paint. This is no jalopy.

ABOVE: Speaking of totally bitchin—and orange—'34 drag coupes, how about this one that is close Ike Iacono's '33 drag coupe to my heart? This is Ike Iacono's original orange-and-black drag car, actually a '33 three window, that first ran a Chevy 6, but is seen here at a car show at Bacon Ford in Hermosa Beach around 1954, featuring a big (320+ cu. in.) GMC inline fitted with what I think is the first aluminum Wayne 12-port head and definitely the prototype Hilborn injectors. He later swapped this engine into his well-known, very fast dragster, which now sits in my garage, fully restored and running with the same head and injector you see here. In '55 this coupe was profusely striped by Von Dutch, then put up for sale (and/or stolen?) a couple years later, less engine, and has never been found since.

BELOW: I mentioned that my photo archive pretty much began with a box full of prints, scratchy negs, timing tags, a scrapbook, Throttle and early Hot Rod magazines, and more given to me by Bill Burke, who briefly worked with me at Street Rodder magazine in the '70s and became a good friend. As a hot rodder he's legendary for many reasons, but probably best known as the inventor of the belly tank lakester. He's seen here in his first version, with a small V8-60 up front and an obviously tight cockpit. His next version was made from a larger tank with the driver in front and a full-size flathead engine in the rear—the Burke-Francisco "Sweet 16," which set several records and became the standard for many others to follow.

BELOW: Speaking of '32 roadsters, including another channeled one (in front), this is a typical line-up at El Mirage in the post-war '40s. The photo was taken by fellow '32 Hiboy owner Jack Mickelson, who was a member of the Vultures car club along with Joe Nitti. The thing to note in this photo is that all three have windshield posts in place, upholstery, mostly nice paint, and even hubcaps, denoting that they were street-driven rods stripped for the weekend races — two with tonneau covers snapped in place to help streamline.

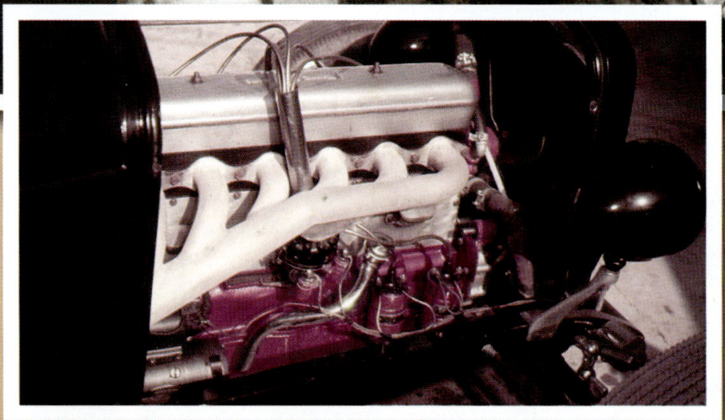

ABOVE & RIGHT: Not too long ago, in my Instagram, I showed a couple B&W photos of Chet Herbert's pretty amazing chopped, fenderless, black '32 Ford Fordor, but I didn't show the engine. Well, during my recent search I found not only some photos of the propane-powered, Horning 12-port head GMC six Chet built for it, but they're in color! Even though he did everything from a wheelchair, Chet was a hands-on builder and incredible innovator who was one of the true hot rod heroes. And you've never seen these photos before, nor will you see them anywhere else.

RIGHT: What, you say, is this? Well…
That's what some readers said when I did
a second, more-tongue-in-cheek Swimsuit
Issue, this one in the Oct. '90 Rod &
Custom. The cars were real (well, most
of them), this of course being the Eddie
Miller handbuilt, Pontiac six-powered
lakester, collected by the Fergusons and
thankfully recently restored. The rest was
pure farce, including captions patterned
after the early Hot Rod "Parts with
Appeal." It all ran in black and white in the
mag, but my favorite photographer (and
good friend) Robert Kittila snapped this
one in color, hoping we'd use it for the
cover. Probably should have.

BELOW: This one is a real mystery. It
came from my shoebox of envelopes
and all it said was Bob Bob Finley '60
T-BirdFinley '60 T-Bird, photos by Bud
Lang. There are several images of the car,
but none showing the rear, engine, or
interior. I figured it was a Starbird custom
– given the look, the bubble top, and the
nice candy red paint. But that little white
thing behind the front wheelwell is an
unrecognizable tag, or emblem, of some
sort. Again doing a brief Google search,
I found a couple references (including
Kustomrama) stating that Bob Finley of
Long Beach, CA, bought Larry Watson's
panel-painted '58 T-Bird in '59. Could this
be the same car? That's all I can tell you.

RIGHT: Here's another good one from the copious Burke files I've never shown before. I can't quite read the license plate date, but I think this was just after the war ('45 or '46). Bill built this T-V8 from a $5 stocker (there are "before" photos). I'd guess it's a Model A frame (with mechanical brakes). It uses later wire wheels, with a filled Deuce grille and headlights. And about the only speed parts for V8s were "slingshot" dual intake manifolds. Bill hand-built the squarish turtle deck, but most significantly he sprayed and rubbed-out a shiny black paint job. Bill always did is own paint, often in his signature "Burple."

BELOW: It was fun to find an envelope full of color photos of Ron Coleman's and his wife's channeled Deuce coupe and chopped '50 Ford custom. I remember reading about them in Hot Rod magazine, where it was emphasized that all work was done in the home garage. Then I got to see them at the first or second Winternationals car show. I was around 13. And it was a thrill to see magazine cars "in person." But even at that age, I remember looking down the sides of the custom and noticing how wavy they were. Coleman had grafted later Oldsmobile quarters and taillights to the rear of the Ford. Interestingly, of the several photos I have, none shows the rear of that car — as here.

RIGHT: It was great to see Jim Govro show up for the AMBR circle at Pomona a year ago with his original Tweedy Bird, looking pretty much like this. You never saw it in a magazine in color back then, but Tom Medley shot this in Texas in '57. Note how the fenders are raised and bobbed on the channeled roadster. Sectioning the stock louvered hoodsides took some real finesse. They cover a detailed Cad V8 with four staggered carbs. I like the matching whitewalls, red wheels, and Olds flipper wheel covers.

LEFT: I've done a couple of columns here called "cover stories." Well, here's another one. We were on a rod run somewhere near Escondido in 1978 when Danny Brent showed up in this wicked, low, very red '29 sedan and I got some good photos of it, which I knew would make a good cover. And I guess I wanted to get it on Street Rodder before somebody else got it. I really can't remember. But the cover caption read: "The paint was barely dry when Ganahl snapped a picture of Danny Brent's new chopped and very louvered '29 sedan. Full feature coming soon." It didn't. Probably because that was my last issue of SRM. But I credit that Model A for instigating the "Red Rod" era that followed shortly.

ABOVE: It was with a pang of sadness that I found these two rough, nearly unprintable images on Hirohata Merca proof sheet of photos I had copied from various people many years ago. Of course I've never shown them before. But these were snapshots Jim McNiel took of his recently acquired (and polished) Hirohata Merc when he was in high school, and of his good-looking new girlfriend Sue, whom he used the Merc to help woo—and marry. They of course stayed that way, and kept the Merc, the rest of their lives. Jim and Sue were wonderful people, and became close friends of both Anna and me. R.I.P. (I would guess the guy in uniform in the upper photo is Jim's older brother Bob.)

LEFT: I don't want to close this lengthy column-for-the-homebound on a down note, so here's my "just one more" photo. As I was refiling proof sheets this one caught my eye. It is, of course Bell Auto Parts, home of Cragar racing components and so much more, in Bell, CA, and I would argue that it was the first, and possibly longest-running, speed shop in the world. You may have seen a similar photo, with different cars in front (including an MG-TC), but this one was taken by a young Tom Medley when he and at least a couple roadster buddies drove all the way down from Oregon, sometime before 1948, to see hot rod sites in SoCal and buy speed parts to take home.

Queenscliff
Rod Run

Words & Photos: Al & Larry O'Toole

ABOVE: Glenn Etchell recently added a bonnet and cool wheel covers on his flathead V8 powered Model A Ford hiboy roadster that also sports twin wind deflectors and red interior trim. In the background is Darren Newton's blue and bumperless '56 Ford F100.

The annual Queenscliff Rod Run is one of the best family rod runs in Victoria, if not Australia, and consistently brings out the best of custom and classic rodding from the southern region. After years of fine-tuning, the Geelong Street Rodders have got the itinerary down pat after hosting the run since 1998.

Queenscliff Recreation Reserve is the venue for the kick-off barbecue on the Friday evening where registration also takes place. Saturday entrants have the pre-selected choice of entry to the Adventure Park complex and a hot dog lunch, or a catered sit-down lunch if you prefer the Saturday cruise option. Saturday night is the popular entrants only street cruise, this year curtailed a little due to cold, rainy weather. Rodders were still out in force enjoying a cruise while most spectators sheltered under the verandahs and awnings of the historic shop fronts that line Queenscliff's Hesse Street.

For 2020 the run attracted 678 entries in total, but that number increased by at least another hundred for the Sunday show and shine. Visitor entry to the show and shine is operated by the Queenscliff/Point Lonsdale Lions Club, with the proceeds all donated to the Lions Bushfire Appeal and wound up being just on $16,000.00!

ABOVE: Dumped '51 Buick lead sled with chopped top and satin black paint belongs to Shannon Jennings. Yes it sits low!

BELOW: Pert hiboy style Model A closed cab pickup has extended cab and small block Chevy engine.
BELOW CENTRE: Phil McNally's low riding Model A Sport Coupe sees regular rod run duty.

ABOVE: Chev Belair station wagon sports wild roof paint and air-bag suspension.

ABOVE: Tidy Chevy 65 Nova SS has potent blown small block engine tucked low in the engine bay is owned by Harley Hamilton.
BELOW: Colin Hill's 1930 Model A Ford Tudor has all of its original style accessories including bumpers and cowl lights.

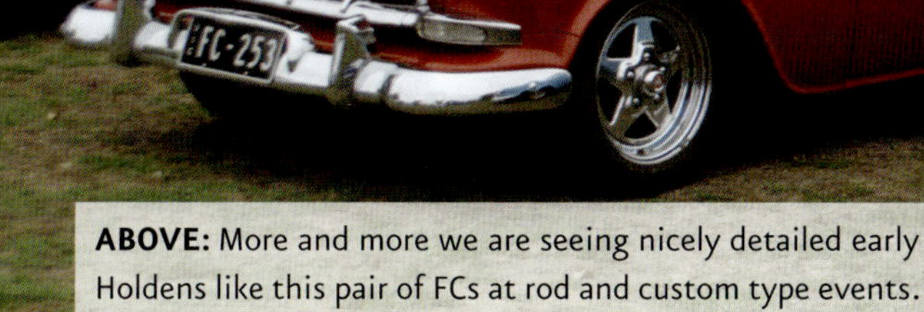

ABOVE: More and more we are seeing nicely detailed early Holdens like this pair of FCs at rod and custom type events. Richard Hall owns the red and white wagon.

LEFT: Wayne Talay owns this outstanding XM Falcon sedan delivery that drew admiring looks all day long thanks to attention to detail and bright metallic orange paintwork with contrasting white roof, plus Cragar S/S wheels.
FAR LEFT: Another wildly painted wagon roof, this time in shades of blue on a '59 Chevy owned by Dale French.

BOTTOM: Craig Smith's convertible Mk I Zephyr exposes its small block Ford V8 engine swap that is so well executed that looks like it came that way from the factory. Note the late model hydraulic struts holding the hood up.

TOP LEFT: The Adventure Park Manager's Choice award went to host club member Terry Pyle's pure white '34 Ford three window coupe.

ABOVE: Mick Grech cruises into Adventure Park on Saturday in his blown small block Chevy powered Model A Ford roadster.

TOP RIGHT: Bayden Roberts' '58 Buick Special just oozes classic American fifties style that it shares with a grey '56 Chevy Nomad and a '64 Mercury.

ABOVE: SLAM-57 is an appropriate plate for this swoopy Buick coupe that sits on chromies and obviously sports air suspension.

ABOVE: Talking of swoopy, they don't come much slicker than this '48 Chevy Fleetline in two tone grey that's been given the full low-rider treatment.

BELOW: Jason Vyner's Model A closed cab pickup always attracts attention thanks to its robust engine and tidy appearance.

ABOVE: Paul Hutchins' '32 Ford five window coupe followed by his Ford pickup cruise the main street of Queenscliff on Saturday night. Cool rainy weather deterred the crowds a bit but the rodders still cruised their hearts out.

RIGHT: Outstanding panel painted theme looks perfect on Sean Hammond's popular '57 Ford Ranchero.

BELOW: Fighter plane themed '33 Ford hiboy roadster of Phil Pieper attracts more then its fair share of attention, thanks to turbocharged small block Chevy engine.

BELOW LEFT: Over from South Australia was Toby Cook in his Datsun powered Anglia.
BELOW: Retro style Ford pickup is a good example of a popular trend in hot rodding.

ABOVE: Bare metal styling with blended graphic on the roof and dumped on the ground suspension ensures Andrew Hodge's '41 Chevy coupe attracts lot of attention at the Sunday show and shine.

ABOVE: Tidy '40 Ford pickup in red oxide sits just right on black steel wheels and lowered suspension. The pickup is owned by Mark Jerinic.
BELOW: It's been around for a while but John Davis' black T bucket still oozes style and class. That's a big block Ford engine sitting behind the stately brass radiator and there's a Jaguar suspension at the other end.

ABOVE: Robert Veitch's '59 Chevy Apache Pickup tucks its large diameter wheels with chrome rims under the fenders thanks to air suspension.
BELOW: American and Australian classics from the sixties. At left is Lisa Dolling's '65 Chevy Belair sedan with Cragar S/S wheels and a '64 EH Holden wagon with surfing theme of the era.

BELOW: Bright yellow paint schemes make this pair stand out. In the foreground is Paul Totevski 1934 Ford Coupe while the 1957 FC Holden ute is Michael Dascoli's vehicle.

LEFT: Dave Monaghan's Top Ten-winning '32 Ford has cowl mounted steering and a superbly dressed 409 Chevy engine with six-carb induction and stylised megaphone headers.

BELOW LEFT: This gasser style '55 Chevy looks "race ready" in white with fenderwell headers, 10 spoke front wheels, typical sign-writing of the era and a Moon tank up front.

BELOW: Slick looking, black four door '32 Ford sedan is one of Gary Brown's fleet of fine street rods.

BELOW: The crowd looks on with admiration as Steven Alldrick heads for home in his "GRNSTR" small block Ford powered hiboy '34 Ford roadster.

BELOW: Leading this line up is the nicely turned out '29 Model A Ford roadster of Ken Clark from Ballarat. It's another small block Ford powered Model A.

BELOW: Early Model A Ford Sport Coupes aren't common, even less so, one that retains original four banger.

ABOVE: Megan Dousset's '36 Ford roadster has been turning heads everywhere it goes since completion. The green roadster has black cloth top, billet wheels and is powered by a 5.7 litre LS1 engine.

BELOW: Chopped '54 Chevy coupe owned by James Chisholm has all the right custom touches such as one-piece bumpers, ground hugging ride height and scallop painted grey bodywork with white roof.

ABOVE: Full fendered '32 Ford roadster sits down snug over its steel wheels with whitewalls combination. Adding to the low profile stance is a dropped headlight bar with stock '32 headlights.

BELOW: Why not bring your David Brown Cropmaster diesel tractor along to the rod run. This restored example was parked up in the main street all weekend where it provided a mini-grandstand view for its owners.

RIGHT: Joe Amato's custom '51 Chevy coupe with doubled up grille attracts the lens of a photographer, keen to catch the effect of the raindrops on the glossy paintwork. Joe's Chevy was a Top Ten winner.

ABOVE: Neville Sunderland has been driving the wheels off his Model A roadster pickup since purchasing it from WA a few years ago.
LEFT: Chrome Joe's Deuce coupe has been around for some time and still looks in perfect condition. Joe Vanutinni gets to drive it to rod runs all over southern Australia on regular occasions.

ABOVE: Peter McVicar's two tone '55 Chevy 210 sedan sports a colour combination not often seen on these models but it suits perfectly and has tinted glass to boot.
ABOVE RIGHT: The chopped '36 Ford three window coupe belongs to George Szulinski and the '32 Ford pickup was entered by Trevor Bartlett.
BELOW: Cruising into the show and shine on Sunday is Kelly Kendall in her show-winning Model A roadster.

ABOVE: Aaron Cole brings his own accommodation to the rod runs, perched on the back of his six cylinder Holden powered roadster pickup.

ABOVE: Host club member Peter Raines cruises the main street of Queenscliff in his bright green, chopped '34 Ford three window coupe.

ABOVE: The show and shine venue is the park immediately below the town centre of Queenscliff where its historic buildings look over the colourful scene. That green Deuce hiboy roadster on the left is big block Chevy powered and the red example on the right is owned by Ron Hutchins.

INSET: Tunnel rammed and black '34 Ford three window coupe of John Mercieca looks like strong performer. It won a Top Ten award too!

RIGHT: Classy '51 Chevy pickup is perfectly finished throughout and powered by a healthy Chevy injected engine. It belongs to Aaron Gregory.

gallery

Ken Senior
Hobby Painter

KEN SENIOR

As a small boy in the '50s I remember the people up the street had a big, old V8 Ford, possibly a Pilot. Apart from my general impression of the car my strongest memory is that one of its rear (laminated?) windows was quite milky. At the time every family near us had English cars, my father had a Vanguard (can I say "sloper"?), so the Ford was something quite exotic.

I am a 1946 Baby Boomer who trained in graphic design and worked as a commercial artist in the 1960s. The late '60s and early '70s involved teacher training and teaching art in secondary schools followed with two year's travel with my wife in Europe, western Asia and North Africa, driving and camping in a Ford Escort van. Back in Australia and further training I returned to teaching, predominately ceramics, in secondary schools. On

OPPOSITE ABOVE LEFT: I painted this for a mate who gave it to his mate (John McLennan, past owner of the cars). I was happy with the result because it was based on two photos on my mobile phone.

LEFT: Ken Senior contemplates another painting.

ABOVE: You may recognize this car which I took from Australian Street Rodding magazine and placed outside the Old Exhibition Building in Melbourne.

TOP LEFT: Completed in 2019 is Alby Olver's '32 roadster (although I didn't know it at the time). It gave me an opportunity to try to paint the reflections of the Old Exhibition Building in the paint. Early on I changed the registration plates of the cars I painted (to protect the innocent) but I've stopped doing that now.

ABOVE LEFT: I painted it after a visit to Murtoa on their 'Big Weekend'. This car show was part of their street market. The grey car had belonged to a rabbit trapper.

retiring I looked for some way to continue my interest in art and making art, eventually settling on drawing and later, watercolour painting. To maintain a steady work rate I have tended to work on themes including factories, city and townscapes, landscapes and since 2018 Hot Rods. I am inspired by the aesthetic qualities of the cars from the '30s and '40s and the modifications made by hot rod and custom builders. In contrast my interest in working on cars is almost zero having, as a young man, spent hours in freezing, smelly garages while my mates worked on their Mini Cooper Ss.

I appreciate the work the owners put into building their cars, although without a background in hot rodding, I have had to refer to the internet to discover the meaning of some of the terms used - "gasser" is still a mystery. I have always been interested in the design and aesthetics of cars but it wasn't until 2018 that I first visited the Hot Rod and Cool Rides show at the Royal Exhibition Building. That and subsequent shows have provided inspiration for my recent work. The number and range of cars, the Exhibition building itself and the rock music have stimulated and provided ideas for paintings. I have tried to express these experiences in my work. Focusing on the shapes of the cars, and reflections in their paintwork, assists me to define the graceful forms of mudguards, hoods, grills etc. Interestingly, the darker coloured and gloss black cars, offer the best reflections. I still find the perspective and multiple ellipses of wheels and capturing the play of light on reflective chrome surfaces an ongoing challenge.

Using my own photos and pictures from ASR magazines I compose drawings to A3 size and paint in watercolour on stretched watercolour paper.   **Ken Senior** ∎

LEFT: Dr L.L. Smith surveying the Cool Rides at the Royal Exhibition Building in Melbourne.

ABOVE: In the car park at the VHRA Show, '36 Ford three window coupe with lots of reflections of the Melbourne summer sky.
BELOW: Outside the Royal Exhibition Building, '34 Ford coupe and Deuce five window coupe.

ABOVE: Possibly my best car and exhibition so far. Changed Rego plate, the original was KOOL I think.

ABOVE: My first attempt to paint a car inside the Exhibition. I found it difficult because there are so many light sources.

FAR LEFT: You will recognize this car from ASR November 2019, but in a different setting.

LEFT: Lyttleton Street west, Castlemaine.

LEFT: This was my first attempt at painting hot rods. It's based on a photo I took at the 2016 Victorian Hot Rod Show. As you can see I used, as a background, Castlemaine's market building.
My connection with Castlemaine goes back to 2002 when my wife and I bought a block of land in Maldon eventually building a weekender. It was during our time up there that I became aware of Castlemaine's importance in the world of hot rodding.

MAIN: You may recognize this picture, it's from ASR May2020. For me it has a subtitle - "a couple of tourists checking out the statue of Dr L.L.Smith M.R.A.C.S. while ignoring the neat '41 Willys".

BELOW LEFT: A real challenge, this painting is subtitled "The Fat Man". BELOW: Composition based on the backs of the Hot Rods & Cool Rides show and the Royal Exhibition Building (and a glimpse of the museum).

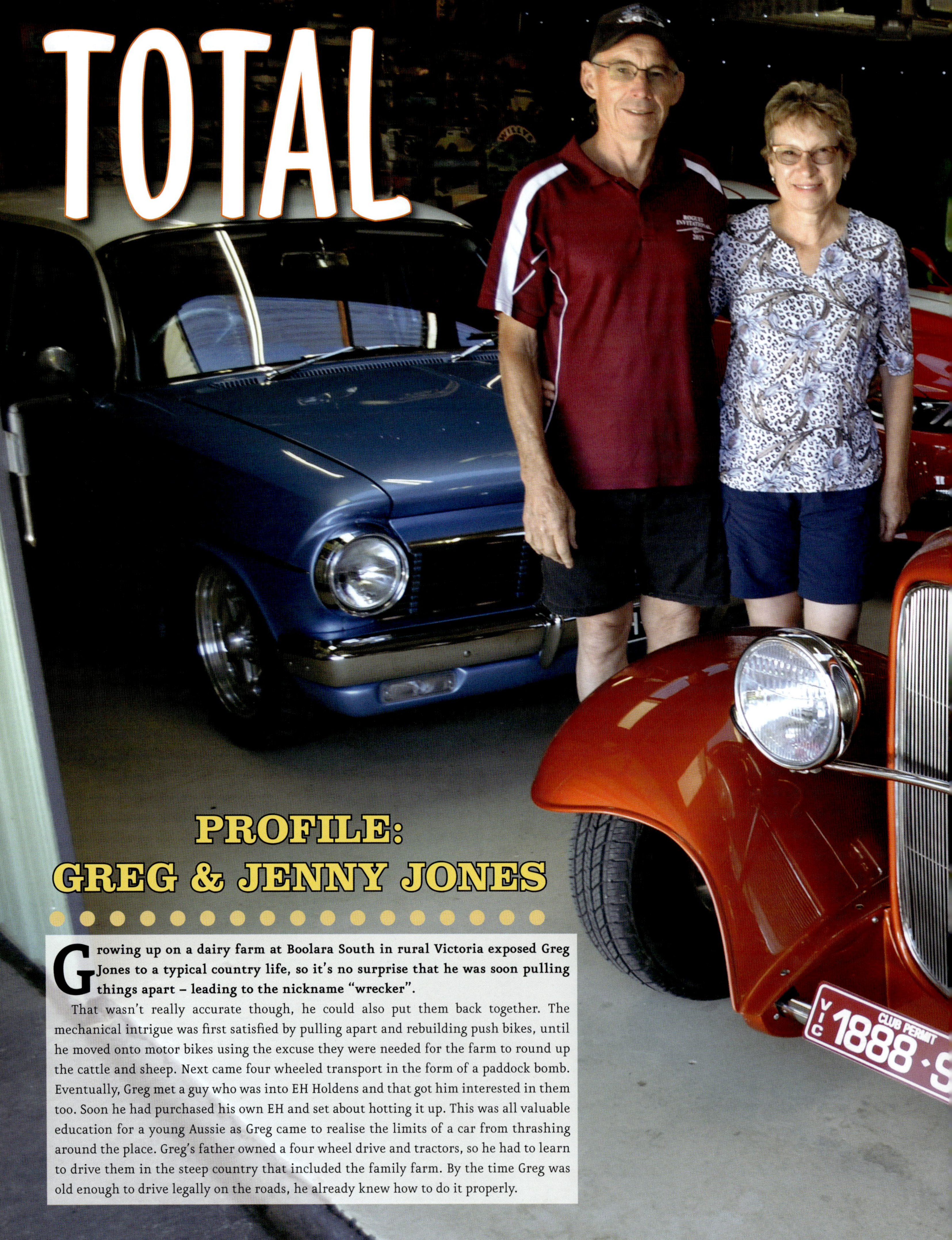

TOTAL

PROFILE:
GREG & JENNY JONES

Growing up on a dairy farm at Boolara South in rural Victoria exposed Greg Jones to a typical country life, so it's no surprise that he was soon pulling things apart – leading to the nickname "wrecker".

That wasn't really accurate though, he could also put them back together. The mechanical intrigue was first satisfied by pulling apart and rebuilding push bikes, until he moved onto motor bikes using the excuse they were needed for the farm to round up the cattle and sheep. Next came four wheeled transport in the form of a paddock bomb. Eventually, Greg met a guy who was into EH Holdens and that got him interested in them too. Soon he had purchased his own EH and set about hotting it up. This was all valuable education for a young Aussie as Greg came to realise the limits of a car from thrashing around the place. Greg's father owned a four wheel drive and tractors, so he had to learn to drive them in the steep country that included the family farm. By the time Greg was old enough to drive legally on the roads, he already knew how to do it properly.

DEDICATION

ABOVE: Greg and Jenny with some of their collection of street rods and classics. The Deuce Tudor was built by Greg for their daughter Andrea. It uses a Deuce Customs body and runs a 383 cubic inch small block Chevy engine. Paint colour is PPG Orange Rock and the interior is trimmed in brown distressd leather.

ABOVE & LEFT: This '34 Ford coupe had been partly channelled, the wheel wells chopped out, etc. It ran a 302 Ford Windsor on straight LP gas with C10 automatic transmission and Centura diff. It rolled on steelies, was built old style and was nice to drive, with semi-elliptics in the rear. The purple '34 was sold to Ian Cornish in Echuca - Victoria and he still owns it.

ABOVE: For a change of pace Greg took on a '41 Willys coupe project that featured a tunnel ram equipped big block 454 Chevy engine, Turbo 400 transmission and nine inch Ford rear end. LPG was the popular way to go at that time, so it was used as the stand alone fuel in the Willys that used a New Zealand made fibreglass body. The coupe was sold to Graham Matthews in South Australia who still owns it today.

LEFT & BELOW: "Fuggly" was another trend-setter from Greg's home workshop in '96. The basket-case body was cleaned up with extended rear fenders and beaver panel, hidden door hinges, smooth repro grille and hood side panels, plus permanently closed windshield. Blue Purple paint even covered the pulled in bumpers. Engine was 350 Chevy on LPG, transmission Turbo 700R and rear end a nine inch Ford. Ted Hogno trimmed it in blue polyester weave fabric over Mazda 929 seats.

Drama intervened when the EH caught fire and Greg tried to save it – the fire was under the floor, so he headed for home to put it out, but didn't make it. Ultimately Greg had to pull over and dive out. He suffered severely burned legs that required skin grafts.

Having trashed the EH, Greg then set about transferring the engine and wheels into a HR Holden that he bought from a local farmer. That was followed by a Mazda Rotary for a while, before Greg headed off to work in Western Australia.

"I came back from WA in 1975 with an FB sedan that had a hot grey motor fitted and drove it for a while. Rust got to it, so down the gully it went with a few other cars, and I bought a HQ Holden wagon powered by a 253 V8. Then I went to Rainbow in Northern Victoria, working at cutting up railway lines. While there I found a '34 Plymouth sedan that I was able to buy for $600.00. I rebuilt it well enough that it became a reliable car, while retaining its original running gear. We used that car for our wedding."

By this time, firmly engrossed in the modified car culture, Greg bought a '35 Ford pickup from Ray Pearman, had it painted, and took it to the 1981 ASRF Street Rod Nationals in Mildura. It was fitted with a 283 cubic inch Chevy engine, Holden front end and HQ Holden diff.

"After it was sold, my attention turned to a '34 Chev roadster that I bought in parts and built up with a 327 Chevy engine. I painted that car myself and always did my own panel, paint and chassis work from then on."

The Chev went to a new owner in Geelong and Greg bought a half disassembled '32 Ford sedan off Con Mantzaris, the former Tony Kuchel '32, that he rebuilt and took to the Nationals. The motor was bad, so the car was rebuilt and the wood framing replaced. Greg kept the Jag rear end and Holden front end, completely steeled out the body and painted it blue. It went to the Canberra Street Rod Nationals, but Greg decided he didn't like the colour, so he painted it again, this time in burgundy and then sold it to a new owner in Warragul.

"Just before selling the '32 sedan, I bought a '37 Ford coupe from Harvey Enchelmaier in Queensland. I went up by bus and drove the '37 home. I still had the '32 for sale, but it didn't sell quickly, so I sold the '37 coupe instead in order to buy a block of land. Then the '32 sold too, and we were able to buy the land. I built a big shed and the house and eventually bought a '32 Ford Tudor from John Cain. It was flat packed on a pallet as it had been cut into squares. I put it back together, painted it and fitted Cleveland running gear. This was the car that won Top Car at Narrandera, then repeated it at Bright in 1991. This '32 Tudor is still around, I sold it to a South Australian owner

ABOVE: A fibreglass '33 Ford three window coupe was next, again based on a Deuce Customs body, but this one had a 350 Chevy engine with Turbo 400 transmission and the old favourite, nine inch Ford rear end. For comfort this one included air conditioning and air-bag suspension. Orange steel wheels and a licking set of flames made it a real stand out and resulted in many Top Car awards at various rod runs.

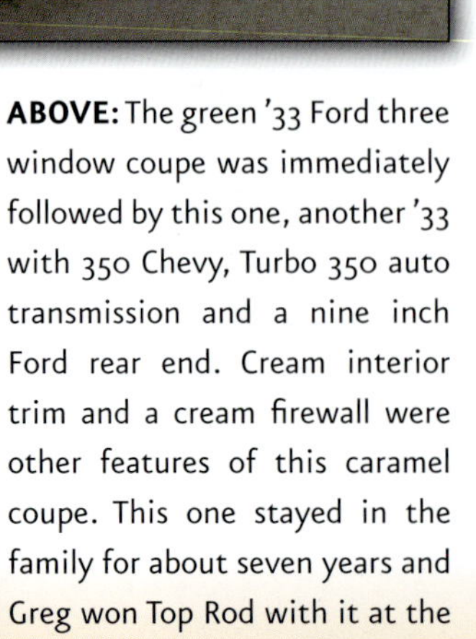

ABOVE: The green '33 Ford three window coupe was immediately followed by this one, another '33 with 350 Chevy, Turbo 350 auto transmission and a nine inch Ford rear end. Cream interior trim and a cream firewall were other features of this caramel coupe. This one stayed in the family for about seven years and Greg won Top Rod with it at the 2009 ASRF Nationals. This coupe is still with its new owner.

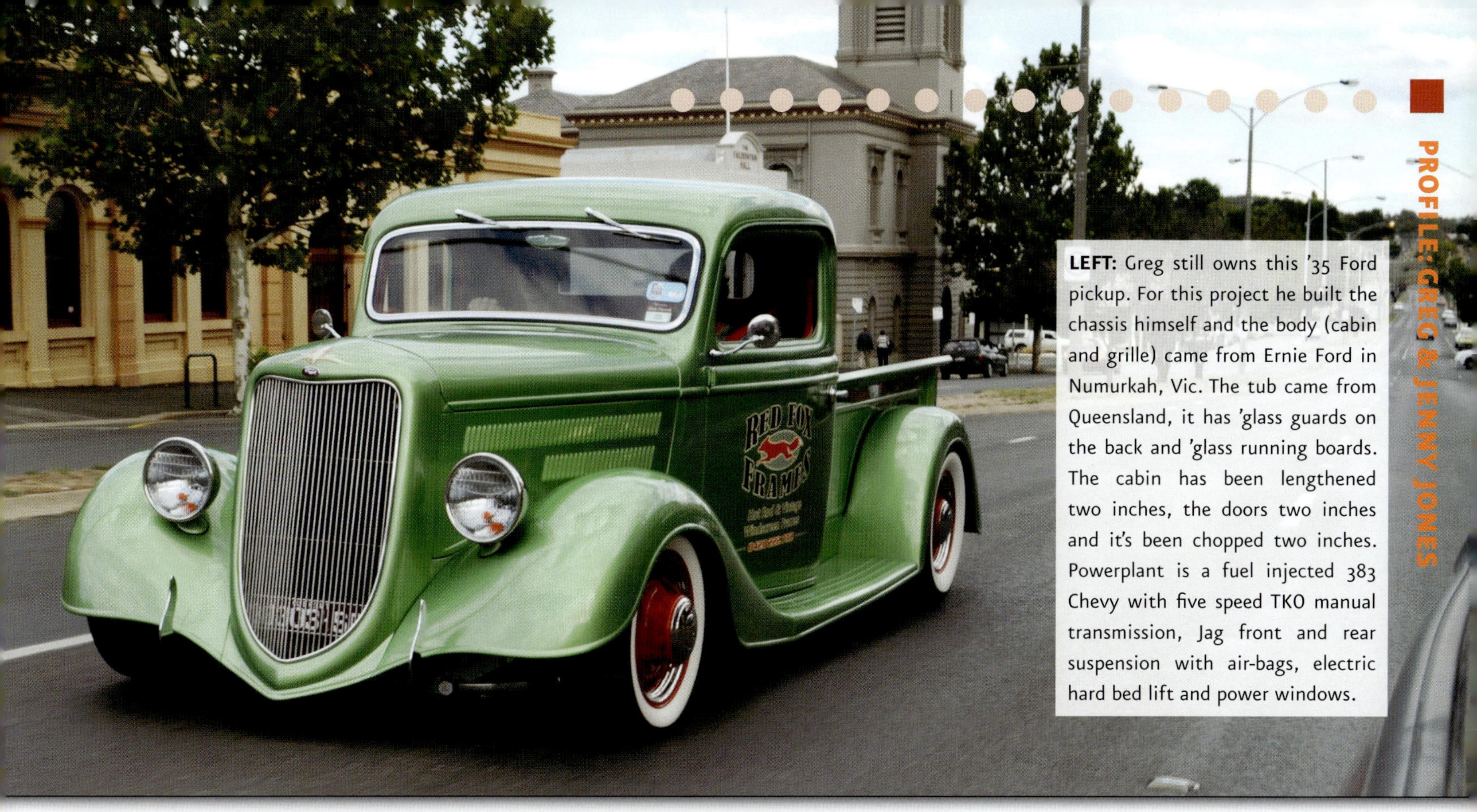

LEFT: Greg still owns this '35 Ford pickup. For this project he built the chassis himself and the body (cabin and grille) came from Ernie Ford in Numurkah, Vic. The tub came from Queensland, it has 'glass guards on the back and 'glass running boards. The cabin has been lengthened two inches, the doors two inches and it's been chopped two inches. Powerplant is a fuel injected 383 Chevy with five speed TKO manual transmission, Jag front and rear suspension with air-bags, electric hard bed lift and power windows.

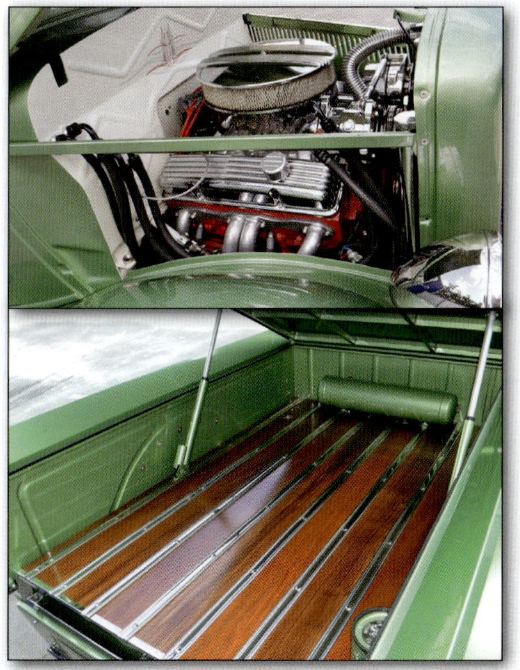

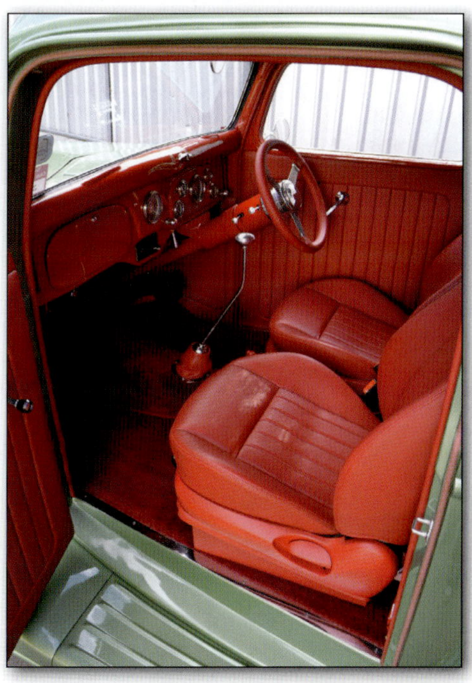

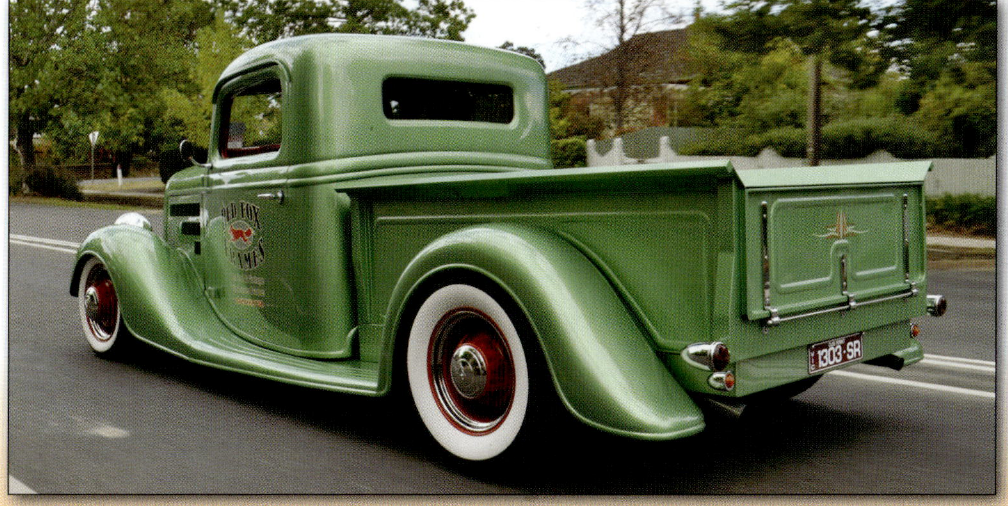

who kept it 10 years. I don't know where it is now but it is still around."

Following the '32 Tudor, Greg bought a really rough '37 Ford coupe that he built into his well known "Fuggly" with TPI Chevy 350 on straight gas, four speed auto, Holden front end and a nine inch diff. It was painted the trendy mono lilac colour in a pastel shade that was popular at the time and won Top Five at Bright Rod Run a few times, Narrandera etc. It was nice to drive, comfortable and had room for the growing kids.

"I bought a '34 Ford coupe off Barry Reynolds that had been partly channelled, the wheel wells chopped out, etc. This one ran a 302 Ford Windsor on straight LP gas, with C10 automatic transmission and Centura diff. It rolled on steelies, was built old style and was nice to drive, with semi elliptics in the rear. That one was sold to Ian Cornish in Echuca and he still has it. I kept the '37 coupe for a couple more years."

A change of direction for Greg saw him embark on a'41 Willys coupe project next. It used a New Zealand made fibreglass body. Fuggly was sold and Greg fitted a 454 big block Chevy with T400 transmission and nine inch Ford rear end into the Willys. It ran on straight LP gas, using twin mixers on a tunnel ram manifold with a Hilborn scoop. It was nice to drive, so Greg and Jenny took it to Valla, then sold it to Graham Matthews in the South Australian Riverland.

"It was time for another coupe so I ordered

The green car photo (full width at top)

ABOVE: Greg had a hand in much of Bob Pankhurst's '36 Ford three window coupe that was the ASRF Nationals Top Street Rod winner in 2005. Greg radically reworked the chassis to accept air-bag suspension and was responsible for cleaning up the bodywork that is devoid of any brightwork. Greg also painted the coupe in Gyco Pearl Green over which ghost flames were added by Acme Signworks. The 350 Chevy powered coupe was set up to run straight LPG through a Corvette TPI manifold and caused a sensation when it first appeared. Bob still owns the coupe that has been driven everywhere since day one.

ABOVE: Son, Steven's ute was built from the remains of a '35 Ford. Initially destined for the tip, Greg said he'd take it and let Steven make something of it. The body had been cut in pieces and the quarters were bent and twisted, but he did make something of it after a lot of hard work and help from dad. The roof was chopped two inches, the door pillars slanted and the firewall recessed to accommodate a 283 Chev engine and Turbo 350 automatic transmission.

a 'glass three window Deuce Customs '33 body, built the chassis myself and fitted a 350 Chevy, Turbo 400 transmission and nine inch rear end with airbag suspension all round. It was even air-conditioned and we kept it for three-four years – same guy that bought it in 2006, still owns it today.

It was immediately followed by another '33 Ford three window coupe with 350 Chevy, Turbo 350 auto transmission and another nine inch Ford rear end. That one we kept for about seven years, before I built the '35 Ford pickup. This one I built the chassis for myself and the body (cabin and grille) came from Ernie Ford in Numurkah. The tub came from Queensland, it has 'glass guards on the back and 'glass running boards. The cab has been lengthened two inches, the doors two inches and it's been chopped two inches. Powerplant is a fuel injected 383 Chevy with five speed TKO manual transmission, Jag front and rear suspension with air-bags, electric hard bed lift and power windows. It's really nice to drive and we still have it."

The next project is an American five window '33 Ford coupe that Greg has owned since 2003. Over the years he has gathered parts, bought a chassis from Harcourt, a grille in the USA from the Early Ford Store and a Rootlieb bonnet. The body is made up from pieces that Greg bought from Fran Kealy who imported it. Greg tried to sell this coupe body at one stage, but it was too much work for most people. Now it's nearly finished. COVID gave Greg the time in the shed to get a lot of work done while there were no events to attend.

ABOVE: The chassis was stripped to the outer rails then boxed and fitted with tubular crossmembers. A HT front end was used and at the rear a diff from a Centura. Front brakes are P76 discs with Falcon XY drums on the rear. The master cylinder is XB Falcon with a homemade pedal assembly. A Falcon steering box was used together with Holden steering arms. The chassis and body has been painted in a home mix of orange pearl two pack paint, while the interior is trimmed in two tone grey vinyl.

ABOVE: Three photos of Greg's '34 Plymouth sedan that started him in hot rodding. The middle photo is of Greg and Jenny returning from Rainbow, Victoria, with the Plymouth in tow. The car evolved but only got to primer stage and was sold. It used 283 Chevy engine, Powerglide trans, plus Holden front end and diff.

ABOVE: The '32 Ford sedan Greg bought from Con Mantzaris around 1984. Greg did a major rebuild, changing it from black to blue, then another colour change a couple of years later to burgundy. The car was sold about 1989. This is the same car that was originally owned by Tony Kuchel in the South Australian Barossa Valley in the late 1960s. When Greg owned it, the running gear consisted of 283 Chevy, Turbo 400, S type jag rear and Holden front end.

ABOVE: This photo of Greg's bronze '35 Ford pickup dates from 1980. It was another 283 Chevy powered car with Powerglide transmission, HT Holden front end and one tonner rear end.

ABOVE: Next was this '34 Chev roadster that Greg built in 1982, this time with a 327 Chevy, Turbo 350, HR Holden front end and '56 Chev diff. It's currently owned by Ray Bedson from Geelong.

ABOVE: In 1994 Greg ventured over into later model territory again with this HQ Holden Kingswood getting a full rotisserie rebuild. This one had 253 V8 and Trimatic transmission.

ABOVE & RIGHT: This bluey-purple '33 Ford American five window coupe came out of Argentina. Greg did a significant amount of the setting up and paint work on this one for John Rech. It was mounted on a Rod City chassis and required lots of replacement bodywork.

ABOVE: Irridescent green '34 Ford coupe used a Deuce Customs body and went together about 2006 for Dave Mathieson. It featured a twin tunnel ram equipped small block Chevy set up to run on straight LPG, a common arrangement at the time, plus a Holden front end grafted into the chassis.

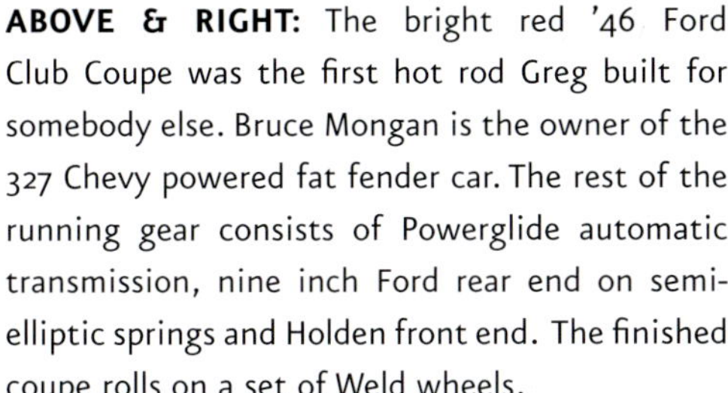

ABOVE & RIGHT: The bright red '46 Ford Club Coupe was the first hot rod Greg built for somebody else. Bruce Mongan is the owner of the 327 Chevy powered fat fender car. The rest of the running gear consists of Powerglide automatic transmission, nine inch Ford rear end on semi-elliptic springs and Holden front end. The finished coupe rolls on a set of Weld wheels.

ABOVE & LEFT: After Greg had finished his blue '32 Ford Tudor, he was asked if he would rebuild Max Godenzi's '33 Ford roadster, shown as it looked as an old hot rod in the 1960s above left, but it was just a body and chassis when Max brought the roadster to Greg. Built from scratch, the hiboy ran a 302 Windsor, C4 transmission, nine inch diff, dicky seat and a Carson style lift-off roof. Max sadly past away a few years ago, but the car still remains in the family and gets used regularly.

ABOVE & LEFT: Greg painted the burgundy '34 Ford coupe for Helmut and Cactus Lirsch in the late 1980s, then in the mid 1990s they wanted to change the whole car, so Greg was called on again to fully rebuild it to how you see it here in yellow. It retained the supercharged small block Ford running gear in both versions but with a hood covering the engine bay when yellow.

Waiting in the workshop is a '35 Ford coupe that Greg bought from Bendigo in 2003. He has already aligned the chassis to sit the whole car lower, increasing the step at the rear in the process to maximise the low stance. This will be a long-term project that Greg will dabble with in between times. He also has an EK Holden Station Wagon project in the wings.

In between all of these street rod projects Greg has managed to build several rods for other people and a couple of Australian classics for himself. The current EH Holden he bought as a going car had been done up in the 1980s with 202 running gear. He drove it for a while, then changed things to get it to ride better. It soon turned into a rotisserie rebuild, the 202 was rebuilt with roller rockers, a Borg Warner diff was fitted and it was repainted. Kool Trim retrimmed the interior using Mazda bucket seats and Greg incorporated EJ Holden stainless interior trim bits, because they look better than the EH version. Later Greg changed the front end to a Rod-Tech independent version with rack and pinion steering. Greg's other classic is another Holden, this time a HT Kingswood.

"The HT was a good body with hardly any rust that I bought off eBay. I wasn't the highest bidder, but the other guy didn't want it, so I got it for less. It had rust in the doors, but a good set came in the deal. I removed the 253 engine and fitted an LT1 fuel injected Chevy, four speed auto and a Borg Warner shortened diff. I tried to fit power steering, but it wouldn't sit low enough, so I fitted another Rod-Tech front end with power steering incorporated. The HT has air-conditioning, Monaro bits including bonnet, guards, dash and console. Once again Kool Trim worked their magic inside using Ford bucket seats. This was another rotisserie rebuild allowing the underside to be as nicely finished as the top. It is a really nice car to drive.

The EK will be next – on a full chassis with six litre Commodore V8, six speed auto and Rod-Tech front end. The body will be stock, rebuilt to include Jenny's choice of colour and billet wheels. It will also get air-bag suspension as it has to sit on the ground."

Passion for the hobby is what has driven Greg Jones to complete so many project cars over the years, but he couldn't have done it without the unfailing support of Jenny. No doubt there will be many more projects to come as the passion is still very much alive.

∎

ABOVE: A recent Jones' built project is this '32 Ford Tudor for daughter, Andrea. This one started out as a coupe but a growing family saw the coupe body substituted for a fibreglass Deuce Customs repro Tudor item as seen here. The chassis has a two inch step in the rear over a nine inch rear end with 3.25:1 ratio gears, while the front suspension is a Rod-Tech independent unit with Commodore brakes and rack and pinion steering. Paint is PPG Orange Rock and the engine is a Tommy Easton built 383 Chevy. Transmission is a Turbo 700 with a Lokar shifter and the wheels are painted steelies fitted with BF Goodrich tyres. The 'glass body has a working original style cowl vent. Adrian Morgan of Kooltrim did the distressed leather interior trim over Mazda 3 front seats and a Holden Rodeo rear seat. Classic Instruments fill the dash, there's a Vintage Air unit underneath and a Flaming River wheel topping the tilt column. Greg used an EZ Wiring harness kit to hook up the electrical components that include Mini Minor cable driven wipers.

ABOVE: Back at the start of this century, Greg built this smart looking '31 Model A Ford Sport Coupe for Terry Deppeler, who lives nearby. The project started out with just the cowl, two doors and rear section of an Argentinian import. Several local rod building businesses were involved in the project with Greg responsible for the bodywork, paint and general assembly. Running gear consists of a 351 Cleveland that has been bored and stroked to 378 cubic inches backed with an FMX automatic transmission and nine inch rear end. The Sport Coupe has an individual style thanks to the use of '28-'29 Model A fenders and a Deuce grille. Paint colour is Yellow Blaze.

RIGHT & BELOW: Rita and Markus Bütler live in the foothills of the Swiss Alps and are big fans of American and Australian vintage cars. During a trip to Australia, they met the Jones family and told Greg about their dream to own an Aussie built hot rod. Greg offered to build them a Pro-Street style 1932 Ford Coupe in tangerine pearl. The careful building to its completion included the exchange of hundreds of emails over a period of almost four years. A few days before Christmas 2008, the car arrived safely in Switzerland after a seven-week-long ship journey. The Bütlers were ecstatic with their new small block Chevy powered Deuce coupe.

LEFT: The chassis for the '35 Ford coupe is already under way, even though this is to be a longer term project. It has been re-aligned through the middle so that it drops the body down over the rails (see photo at bottom right of opposite page) and given an extra kick up over the rear end so that it can be equipped with air-bag suspension and dropped very low in typical Jones fashion.

BELOW: Front sheetmetal is notoriously difficult to get aligned on these '35 Fords but this one is already done!

BELOW: A fairly tidy original '35 Ford Tudor body waits in the background as the EK Holden wagon on the foreground will be Greg's next project. It will get another Rod-Tech independent front end, along with six litre Commodore engine and six speed transmission. Jenny will dictate choice of colour and billet wheels. The body will remain entirely stock but will be capable of being dropped on the ground thanks to another full air-bag suspension system. The EK is in very good condition for its age, but will be treated to a full rotisserie rebuild in Greg's home based workshop.

ABOVE: Here's another look at that '35 Ford Tudor body and the back half of the '35 Ford coupe that Greg recently started work on as shown in the photo at right. The chassis has been radically reworked (see original profile) to allow it to sit very low, but still has plenty of clearance over the rear end. Greg's huge home workshop is well equipped with all the tools required to build projects like this from scratch and even includes a paint booth for painting them when finished.

RIGHT & BELOW: You won't find a better HT Holden Kingswood on the planet! Greg gave this one a full rotisserie rebuild, outfitted it with a Chevy LT-1 engine from a Corvette with 4L60E transmission and Falcon Borg Warner disc brake LSD rear end. Externally the HT has had its appearance smartened up with Monaro bonnet and fluted front guards. Underneath is yet another Rod-Tech independent front end with power rack and pinion steering. Interior trim is all grey vinyl with darker grey pleated inserts by Kool Trim and there's air conditionin to make summertime travelling as comfortable as a modern car.

BELOW: Parking for some of the finished cars is in this front section of the shed where we find Greg and Jenny's superbly rebuilt EH Holden and the green '35 Ford pickup separated by their late model hack - a current model Ford Mustang. The walls are extensively decorated with all manner of automobilia, collected mostly from swap meets over the years they have been involved in the hobby.

BELOW & RIGHT: Almost finished is Greg's latest project, another '33 Ford coupe. This time he used an original American steel five window body that he had tried to sell, but it was too much work for most people. Greg decided he would fix it himself and fully build it as his next project. As you can see in these photos, it is going to be another beauty with Chevy W motor in the engine bay and air-bag suspension all round. Check out the low, low stance in the bottom photo on this page and the perfect pearl brown paintwork. The body required extensive steeling out and a complete new floor as you can see in the photo at right.

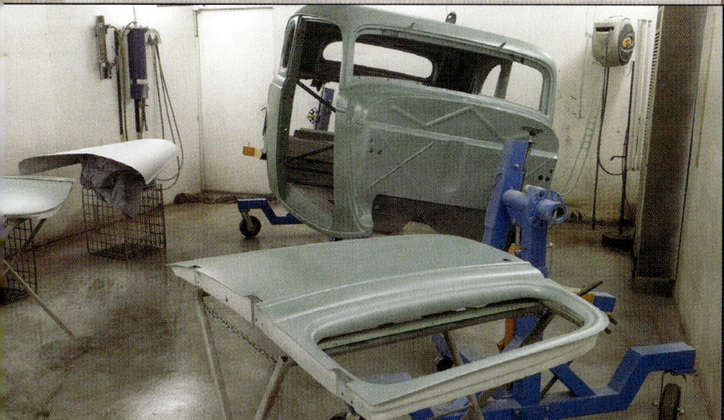

RIGHT & BELOW: The EH Holden sedan retains a 202 red six engine equipped with twin X2 carbies, Yella Terra head with roller rockers and is mated to a five speed Toyota Celica manual transmission. The inside is trimmed in Mercedes style coffee vinyl over Mazda bucket seats in the front and with EJ stainless steel trims on the door panels and an original accessory louvre blind in the rear window. Under the back of the EH is a Falcon Borg Warner LSD rear end, this one equipped with drum brakes. Vintage Air supplied the air conditioning unit for the EH that was an orignal Premier. Once again Greg used a Rod-Tech independent front end with disc brakes and power rack and pinion steering.

BOTTOM: A huge enlargement of a photo of the green '35 Ford pickup and the caramel '33 Ford coupe adorn the upper wall of Greg's "man-cave", along with show signs and other general automobilia. You can tell that Greg and Jenny's rods get driven by the number of participant number plates in the collection at the bottom of the photo.

OPPOSITE PAGE: Greg's relaxation retreat is his "man-cave" in the shed that, apart from being suitably decorated, is also air-conditioned, so the whole family tends to spend a lot of time in there during the summer months.

PROFILE: GREG & JENNY JONES

MOONEYES
Hot Rod Custom Show

Story: Al & Larry O'Toole
Pics: Darron Davies

MAIN: Mr. Ito's '39 Dodge "Kona Gold" Super Chop Custom built coupe, winner of Best Suede and Max Grundy's Pick.

TOP LEFT: Enthusiastic crowd try to capture the roll-in of the guest participants soon after the show opened.

LEFT: Tail draggin' '59 Chevy Pickup of Mr Matsumaru from Square Kustoms was awarded the Best American Pickup trophy.

For several years the Yokohama Hot Rod Custom Show, commonly known as the Mooneyes Show due to Mooneyes owner Shige Suganumi being the principle promoter, has pursued a Keep Calm, Stay Cool theme as it faced closure due to the local community being disrupted by noise from the large crowds going to and leaving from the show. This approach worked and the show was able to continue, but everyone is aware of not reverting to the noisy ways, so that the show can continue well into the future. Hot rod and custom enthusiasts travel from all around the world to be part of this event, in fact 1900 of them, according to the official Mooneyes website, and they joined with 19,000 local Japanese patrons to see one of the best car show spectacles in the world.

For international visitors, even the set up day is a must and it concludes with a pre-show party for everyone involved. When the doors opened at 8:00 am on December 1 there was a huge crowd waiting to spill into the Pacifico Exhibition Centre, right on the Yokohama waterfront. The show is one day only, so the activity level is frenetic all day long. The "Ride-In" starts at 9:00am when the invited guests parade into the show in their special exhibit vehicles and the crowd mills 10 deep either side trying to get the best photos. Then each guest is interviewed and autograph signing follows.

On the floor, the show is divided up into various categories, this year including the Hot Wheels Collector Convention, the International Village vendor area, Scale Model section and Pinstripe Gallery. Four bands provided live music, there was a Pin-up Competition and a Slip-on Shoe Painting comp thanks to the involvement of Vans.

If you have never been to the Mooneyes Show, add it to your bucket list right now.

TOP RIGHT: "Best of '70s" went to Mr. Harada of Van Nuys Automotive for his green with pinstripes S/S drag racing 1974 Ford Maverick called "Drag'n Fly".

RIGHT: That's the original colour on this 1964 Ford Ranchero Falcon Ranchero with black flames added over the top.

CLOCKWISE FROM LEFT: "Best of '50s" and Fly Wheels Magazine's Pick went to the 1950 Plymouth Special Deluxe owned by Mr. Kagei. · Pumpkin Sally is a chopped and restyled '30 Model A Ford coupe with Deuce grille and clear coated bare metal finish. · Unique blue '37 Ford three window coupe is based on an aftermarket concept as Ford never made such a bodystyle. Note the extensive use of custom made polished trim. · The gold 1940 Mercury won Best of '40s for Wheels Unlimited. · Patina covered '41 Chevy sedan delivery from the Killers of Silent Hll looks barn fresh right down to the "Approved GM Accessories" sign.

TOP LEFT: Displayed on the Flames stand was this appropriately decorated '58 Pontiac coupe with chopped top, kustom front end treatment and billet American wheels.
TOP RIGHT: Another Chevy, this time the chopped '54 Belair coupe from El Classico Vintage and Antiques.

MAIN: Produced by Richard Zocchi this 1962 Pontiac Grand Prix "Creamsicle" with current owner/driver John D'Agostino was one of several guest exhibits to come to the Mooneyes Yokohama Hot Rod Custom Show from the USA.

RIGHT: Hyo Do Katsumi owns "El Pantera Negro", a 1967 Chevelle with ghost flames that runs a 364 cubic inch LS engine with a 4L65E transmission and red and black interior trim.

LEFT: Pink 1965 Buick Le Sabre exhibits some subtle cusotm touches and a superb Gene Winfield fade-away paint scheme.

BOTTOM LEFT: Red and white 1957 Ford Fairlane convertible was the Mitzi's Pick, Chevy Service, Miki award winner for owner Mr. Mitsuda. Lakes pipes and red on white contrasted with white on red pinstriping highlights are just a few of the outstanding features.

BOTTOM: Mooneyes Sweden's Pick went to Kazuya Ito's aluminium-bodied 1929 Model A Ford based race car that looks like it came straight from that era's Indianapolis 500.

ABOVE LEFT: Best American Car, Deuce Factory trophy winner was Mr. Kasai's 1932 Ford American Graffiti clone coupe with all the right appointments right down to the chrome wheels.

ABOVE: Best Custom, DX Magazine's Pick K-Line went to this 1981 Mitsubishi Debonaird custom that displays well executed panel paint scheme and continental kit at the rear, plus half wheel skirts. Owner is Mr. Aihara.

MAIN: There's a lot to like about the mildly customised 1953 Oldsmobile coupe that shared a stand with Mr Ito's "Kona Gold" 1939 Dodge coupe. This photo was taken during set-up time on the Saturday to which international guests are invited, giving them an inside look at the show behind the scenes. They also get to attend the show party, held in the evening after set-up is complete.

LEFT: Metalflake gold with red accent stripes graces the bodywork of this classic "Hugger" 1979 Camaro that features a "power bulge" hood.

BELOW: Best Kustom, Celebrity Kustoms/John D'Agostino's Pick was the 1940 Mercury Eight El-Classico of Mr. Matsumoto from Vintage & Antiques.

ABOVE: West Aussie rodder, Ben Forster entered his trike known as "Zeitgeist" with radical C cab styling, pattern painting and twin cylinder motorcycle engine.

RIGHT: This '32 Ford Model B Roadster - in memory of Ken Katashio featured a Deuce Factory chassis, Rod Bods body, 383 Chevy engine, Richmond five speed transmission and Halibrand quick-change rear. Best of Show Auto, Burnout Magazine's Pick and Car Magazine's Pick.

ABOVE RIGHT: Another guest car of the show was the "Tweedy Pie" '23 T bucket of Bob Johnston from Anaheim, California. He built the widened bucket in the mid-fifties, had it pinstiped by Ed Roth and then sold it to Roth in 1962. It was featured on the covers of magazines in 1959 and 1962 before Revell issued it as a very popular scale model kit in 1963.

LEFT: On the Quatro Cinco Kustom Style stand was this matte finished, chopped and dropped single spinner Ford coupe.

BELOW: Best of "Experience The Fabulous" Extraordinary & Unusual Kustom and MOONEYES USA's Pick was Mr. Tsutsui's 1962 Pontiac Grand Prix "Grand Blue".

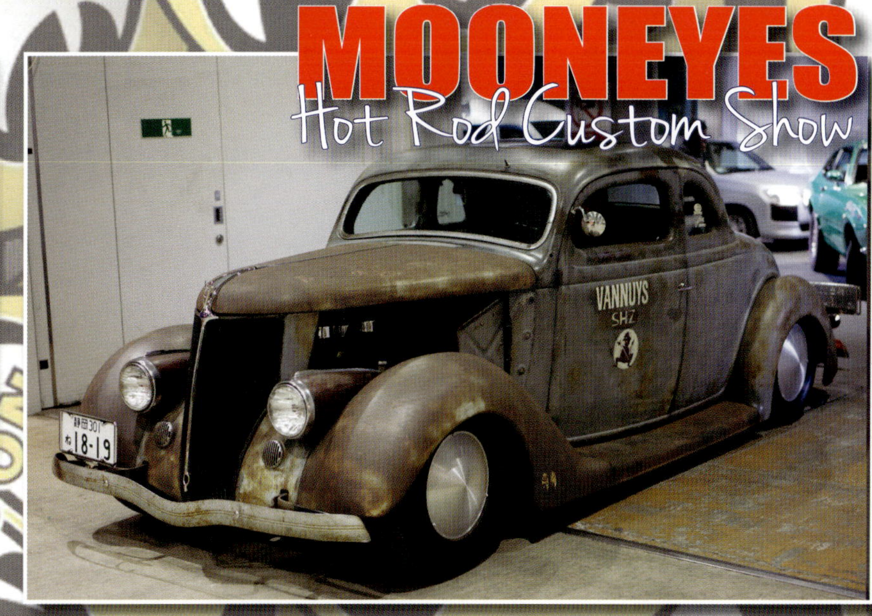

ABOVE: Hiroki Kishiyama's 1950 Chevrolet "Metal Warrior" has restyled bodywork by AutoBody A's. The original design was by Van Nuys Automotive.

ABOVE: Van Nuys Automotive 1936 Ford is chopped and dropped, features non-Ford headlights and "barn find" patina.
LEFT: Guest show car, Bob Reisner's "Bath Tub" 1968 built Show Rod was recently restored by Dave Shuten and driven in by Beau Boeckmann of Galpin Auto Sports.
BELOW Junichi Shimodaira is a regular participant in the Yokohama show with his wildly 'flake painted Galaxian T bucket.
BOTTOM: El Classico Kustoms La Salle coupe has been left in bare metal so you can appreciate the workmanship that has gone into it.

MUSCLE CAR MADNESS

With a highly successful 30th anniversary just last year, followed by the year we have all had, nobody really knew what was in the offing at Muscle Car Madness #31 or even if we could have it. Entries only went out in October due to COVID-19 and we all had our fingers crossed.

We bit the bullet and negotiated to have the "Uncertain T" show car as our main drawcard which was a real hit with the crowd. The other big move was to contract the Jordan Luck band (ex Exponents) as the main band of Friday night for the 1500 competitors camped at the showgrounds. The event kicked off on Wednesday night. Thursday night sees around 300 cars on the twilight "twin towns" tour that takes in Rangiora and Kaiapoi to entice the eager local crowd to the main weekend show that features around 1300 cars on the Saturday. Friday's Classic Covers scenic run headed out to Ashley Gorge fiver for a lunch stop.

Live bands played all weekend, a rockabilly pageant and the famous on site burnout pad kept everyone entertained along with night time camp ground cruising.

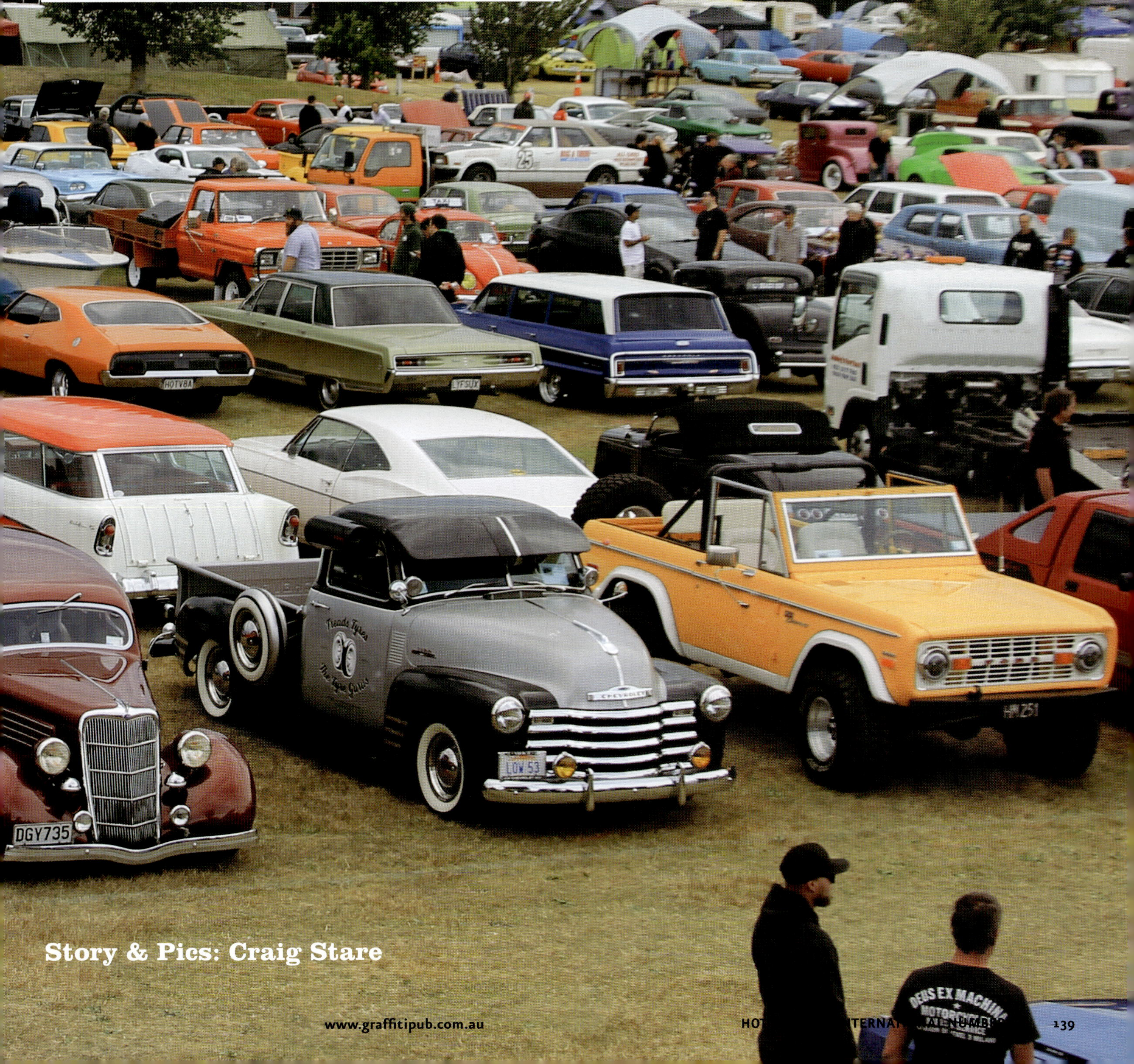

MAIN: A small portion of the cars on show in the main arena on Saturday.

RIGHT: Malcolm Bain drove Justin Little's custom EK ute that was made from a station wagon all the way from Dunedin.

BELOW: Globe wheels look great, so does the blown 408 Cleveland engine. The 1971 Falcon was built by Johnny Miller.

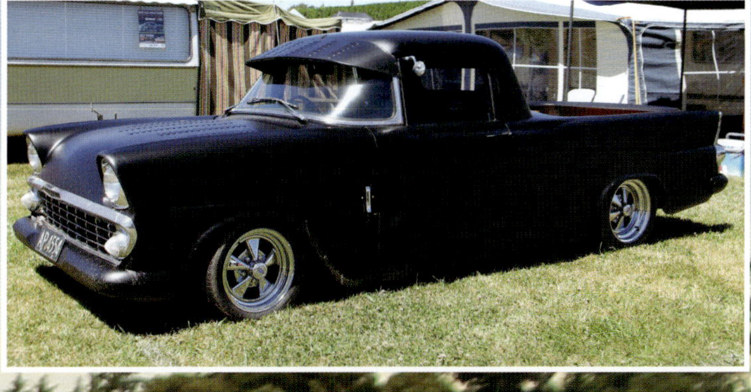

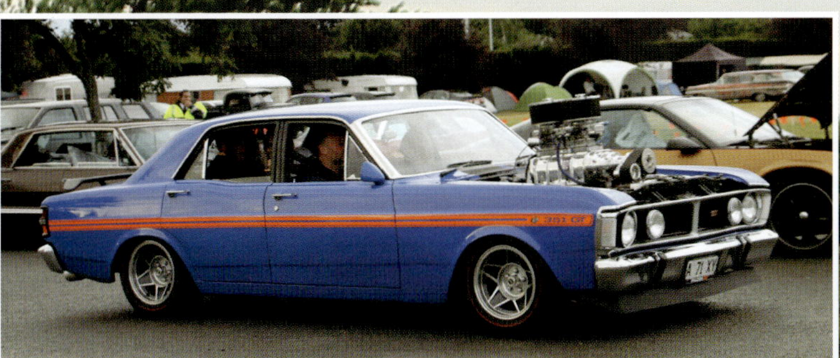

RANGIORA SHOWGROUNDS NORTH CANTERBURY NEW ZEALAND

Story & Pics: Craig Stare

TOP LEFT: Pagan gold 1961 T bird "looks the part". It's low stance and chromies add to the effect owned by Jason Bishop.

ABOVE: Sadly Kim Mitchell recently passed away but the family displayed his perfect 1968 Camaro taking out Best Chevrolet and a Top Ten award.

LEFT: Ian Paki's 1963 Pontiac Catalina looks like a drag strip refugee from days gone by. Hot small block Chev engine propels the cat to mid elevens.

ABOVE LEFT: Neat pink HT Holden Monaro seen on Friday's scenic Ashley Gorge run.

ABOVE: Daniel Rawson and friend Ty drove all the way down from Auckland in this great '33 Ford roadster powered by a 383 Chevrolet and Tremac five speed transmission.

LEFT: Mel Hannon recently moved down from Auckland and soon had many volunteers to be passengers. Her 1959 is slick!

LEFT: Left Matt Love had his swoopy Plymouth Barracuda looking amazing, another great car built by 185 Restorations.

BELOW: Bright blue Falcon ute sounded good and looked evil too. Dave Roberts is the creator.

BELOW LEFT: Just your regular V8 powered street legal mini ute.

RIGHT: Very rare 1958 Edsel Bermuda cruising the camp ground.

BELOW: Craig Stare had several cars on site. The "Indian Turquoise" 1959 Thunderbird sits low and the 1957 Ford Courier had been in the shed for six years, didn't miss a beat.

ABOVE: Garrett Matthews demonstrated lots of blown Chevrolet power in his HQ Holden one ton flatbed ute from Ashburton. This vehicle is a regular at all the south island burnout events.

ABOVE RIGHT: This wild burnout was so sustained it just blew the bumper off the old AU Falcon sedan.

RIGHT: An LH Torana lights up the hides in spectacular fashion during the burnouts!

BELOW: Dillon Orpwood gives the jacked up 1933 Willys gasser coupe the message, a small block Chevy gets it motivated.

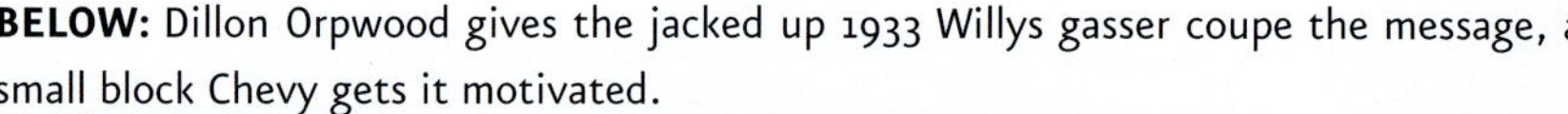

MUSCLE CAR MADNESS

ABOVE: Show car worldwide is Martin Bennett's "Uncertain T" from Cambridge. Last year the car did an extensive USA show tour, winning 20 awards in five different shows! That's a superbly dressed Buick Nailhead V8 adorning the engine bay.

RIGHT: Dwane Wright McLaren went "TOPLSS" and had the plate to prove it with his Falcon wagon.

BELOW: One and half HQ Holden station wagons certainly had people talking.

LEFT: Jonnie Wright and Ang travelled down from Wellington in a finned headed, flathead Ford V8 powered Model A Sport Coupe.

BELOW LEFT: Very rare 1959 Ford two door Ranch wagon was immaculate.

BELOW: Wayne Tierney drove his 1938 Ford coupe down from Wellington.

BELOW: Another very nice 1971 XY Ford Falcon.

RIGHT: Peter Haywood from Gore owns this chopped '32 Ford hiboy coupe and played with it in the dirt all weekend.

RIGHT: Rolling Bones style salt influenced 1934 Ford hiboy three window coupe is owned by Ross Campbell from Nelson. patina paint and wire wheels suit the style.

BELOW: Tony Brunt's "hot pink" HQ Holden has more than enough power to get the job done using blown big block Chevy power.

BELOW RIGHT: Another blower, this time topping the engine in an tuff XC Falcon four door sedan.

BELOW: Some competitors came to show their cars but others like Joel Vincent and his mates preferred to spend their time cruising in his XR Falcon sedan.

RIGHT: Hayden Wilby's "NUTOUT" Holden is an evil burnout car and has even competed at the Summernats in Australia, along with a thumping out a few street miles as well.

BELOW LEFT: A couple of reworked HQ Holden sedans. One has had it's roof amputated, the other has a 6-71 blower sticking out of the engine bay.

BOTTOM: Here's a rear view of Matt Lowe's Plymouth Barracuda that accentuates its swoopy styling.

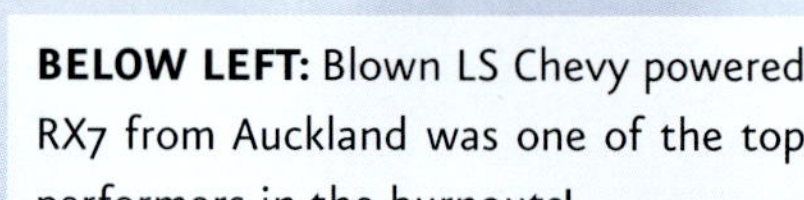

BELOW LEFT: Blown LS Chevy powered RX7 from Auckland was one of the top performers in the burnouts!
BELOW: Local Rangiora man Graham Coates' radical custom Chevy pickup was again one of the winners.

ABOVE: Vans Unlimited displayed a bunch of HQ-HZ Holden panel vans at their amazing drive-in diner display.

RIGHT: On the move is Carl Pender's 1962 Chevy that would look positively evil if you suddenly saw it in your rear vision mirror!

BELOW: Steven Saul cruised this seriously powered drag racing Capri for a few laps but it developed mechanical problems and had to be retired to the sidelines.

AUSSIE DRAG HISTORY

Every so often an old hot rodder drops into our offices with some gem of antiquity that gets everyone excited to know that it still exists. Cue Jack Collins, aka Fizzball from the heady drag racing days of the 1960s, you know, back when it was all fun and the cars were essentially combinations of go-fast goodies of the period put together in rodders' back yards or humble workshops. Jack was the inaugural Top Eliminator at the first Australian Drag Nationals held at Riverside in Melbourne in 1965 when he pedalled Norm Beechey's Holden six cylinder rail to a win over Eddie Thomas' ailing Chrysler powered dragster.

Move on to 1968 and the sport of drag racing had grown and evolved somewhat, but was essentially still a "run-whatcha-brung" activity. Riverside had closed in late 1966 and attention then moved to Calder Raceway where the drag strip part of that operation became reality in early 1968 (see poster). By then Jack Collins had graduated to Meeting Director for the Calder facility and it was he that was in charge for the '68 Drag Nationals scheduled for October 5 and 6 of that year. I say scheduled, because it wasn't actually completed on those dates, wild, windy and finally wet weather curtailed activities before the meeting could be concluded, so they came back and finished the Nationals off in conjunction with Calder's normal monthly meeting in November when the weather was nearly perfect.

So it was that Jack wandered into our office with a bundle of papers in a folder that he thought we might find useful. That bundle of papers was the entire entry list for the 1968 Drag Racing Nationals. What makes an old bundle of entry forms of historical significance? Well a great number of the names on those entry forms went on to become household names in the world of hot rodding and drag racing and better yet, the forms included details on all of the vehicles entered – that in itself makes interesting reading now that we are 63 years deeper into history.

Then it became a project of tracing photos of as many of these drag racing cars as we could dig out of our archives to match them back with their 1968 entry forms. Enjoy the read – and the reminiscing! ■

BELOW: Ray Charlton was a regular competitor at Calder in his Y block Ford powered yellow '32 Ford roadster. He is seen here in action against Peter Leech's flathead powered version with full disc wheel covers and whitewall tyres.

1968 NATIONALS

ABOVE: An early shot of the Calder pits around the time of the '68 Championships.
BELOW: Eddie Thomas was already established as the Big Daddy of Australian drag racing by 1968 when his dragster had evolved to the version shown below, full bodied and with front mounted blower. For the '68 Nationals he moved the blower to the top of the engine as shown in the lower photo and put down the best run of the meet, but he didn't like the blower up top, because he found it difficult to see around. Shortly after he retired from competing at the drags but still retained an interest in all things automotive until his passing at 99 years of age.

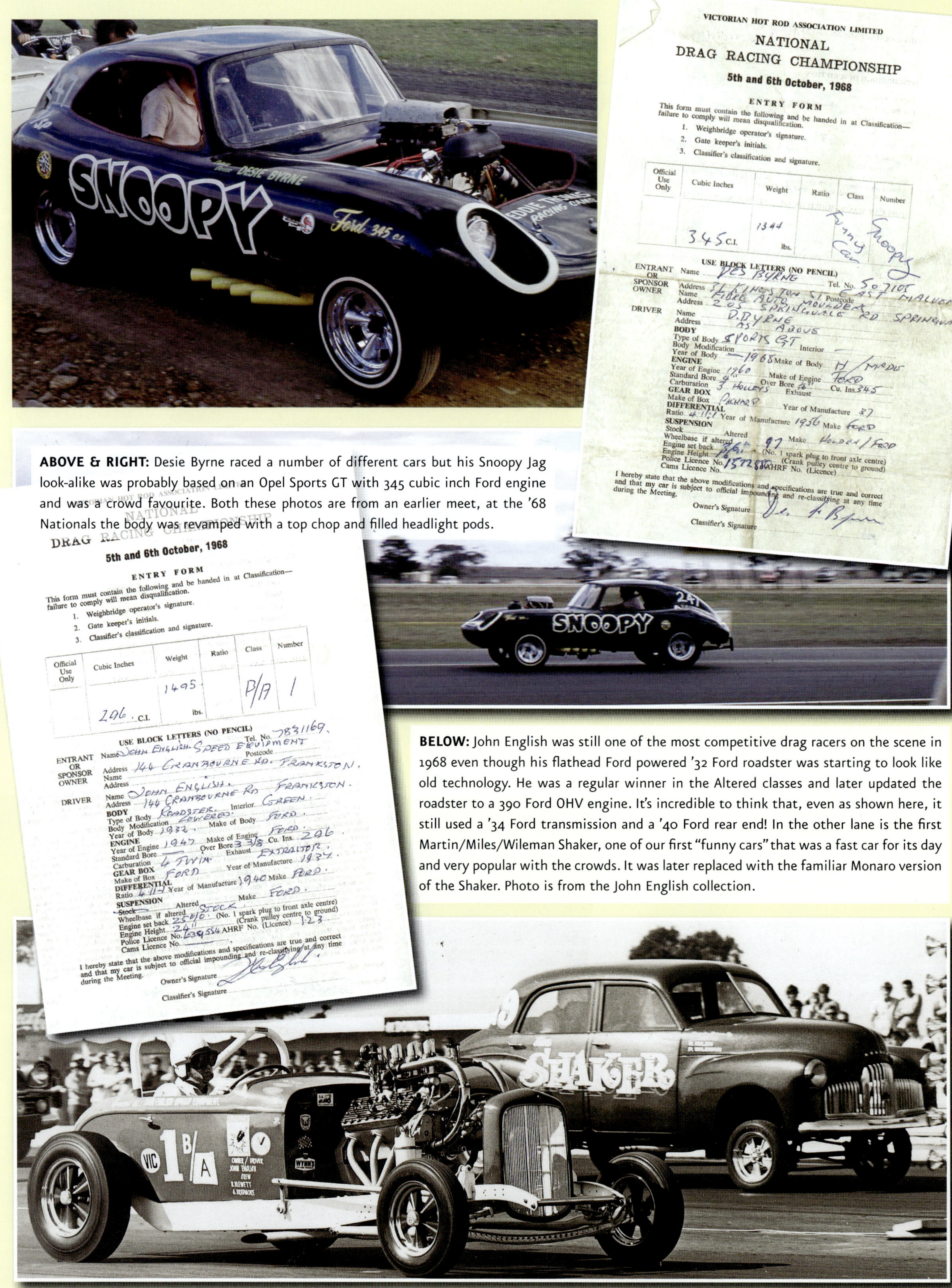

ABOVE & RIGHT: Desie Byrne raced a number of different cars but his Snoopy Jag look-alike was probably based on an Opel Sports GT with 345 cubic inch Ford engine and was a crowd favourite. Both these photos are from an earlier meet, at the '68 Nationals the body was revamped with a top chop and filled headlight pods.

BELOW: John English was still one of the most competitive drag racers on the scene in 1968 even though his flathead Ford powered '32 Ford roadster was starting to look like old technology. He was a regular winner in the Altered classes and later updated the roadster to a 390 Ford OHV engine. It's incredible to think that, even as shown here, it still used a '34 Ford transmission and a '40 Ford rear end! In the other lane is the first Martin/Miles/Wileman Shaker, one of our first "funny cars" that was a fast car for its day and very popular with the crowds. It was later replaced with the familiar Monaro version of the Shaker. Photo is from the John English collection.

VICTORIAN HOT ROD ASSOCIATION LIMITED

NATIONAL
DRAG RACING CHAMPIONSHIP

5th and 6th October, 1968

ENTRY FORM

This form must contain the following and be handed in at Classification— failure to comply will mean disqualification.

1. Weighbridge operator's signature.
2. Gate keeper's initials.
3. Classifier's classification and signature.

Official Use Only	Cubic Inches	Weight	Ratio	Class	Number
	155 C.I.	1100 lbs.		DA	50

USE BLOCK LETTERS (NO PENCIL)

ENTRANT OR SPONSOR OWNER — Name HARRISONS SPEED SHOP — Tel. No. 75 — Address 2 MACKAY ST ROCHESTER — Postcode 3561

DRIVER — Name MAURICE MUNDIE — Address VICTORIA ST ROCHESTER

BODY
Type of Body FIAT (SINGLE SEATER) — Interior
Body Modification GUTTED — Make of Body FIAT
Year of Body 1949
ENGINE
Year of Engine 1961 — Make of Engine Holden
Standard Bore 3½ — Over Bore 3¾ — Cu. Ins. 155 — Exhaust Lukey Burning Branch
Carburation Triple Strombergs
GEAR BOX
Make of Box Holden — Year of Manufacture 1950
DIFFERENTIAL
Ratio 3·89 — Year of Manufacture 1957 Make Holden — Make Ford Prefect
SUSPENSION
Stock Prefect — Altered
Wheelbase if altered
Engine set back (No. 1 spark plug to front axle centre)
Engine Height (Crank pulley centre to ground)
Police Licence No. 1449887 — AHRF No. (Licence) 35
Cams Licence No. Nil

I hereby state that the above modifications and specifications are true and correct and that my car is subject to official impounding and re-classifying at any time during the Meeting.

Owner's Signature *Maurice M. Mundie*
Classifier's Signature

ABOVE: Maurie Mundie ran his quickest time ever at the Nationals with a 12.79 pass in his grey Holden powered Fiat altered. The two pictures are from slightly different eras, note the signwriting and headers.

VICTORIAN HOT ROD ASSOCIATION LIMITED

NATIONAL
DRAG RACING CHAMPIONSHIP

5th and 6th October, 1968

ENTRY FORM

This form must contain the following and be handed in at Classification— failure to comply will mean disqualification.

1. Weighbridge operator's signature.
2. Gate keeper's initials.
3. Classifier's classification and signature.

Official Use Only	Cubic Inches	Weight	Ratio	Class	Number
	298 C.I.	2016 lbs.	A/CR	10	10

USE BLOCK LETTERS (NO PENCIL)

ENTRANT OR SPONSOR OWNER — Name DENNIS BURNS — Tel. No. 379 7963 — Address 66 NEWMAN CRES NIDDRIE — Postcode

DRIVER — Name — Address

BODY
Type of Body "A" PICKUP — Interior
Body Modification SHORTENED — Make of Body FORD
Year of Body 28
ENGINE
Year of Engine 1956 — Make of Engine FORD
Standard Bore 3½ — Over Bore 040 — Cu. Ins. 292 — Exhaust Headers
Carburation 3×2
GEAR BOX
Make of Box Ford — Year of Manufacture 1950
DIFFERENTIAL
Ratio 4·09 — Year of Manufacture 55 Make Ford
SUSPENSION
Stock Ford — Altered 10 Leaf Ins
Wheelbase if altered
Engine set back 10" (No. 1 spark plug to front axle centre)
Engine Height 11" (Crank pulley centre to ground)
Police Licence No. 150504 — AHRF No. (Licence)
Cams Licence No.

I hereby state that the above modifications and specifications are true and correct and that my car is subject to official impounding and re-classifying at any time during the Meeting.

Owner's Signature
Classifier's Signature

ABOVE: A regular competitor in the hot rod classes of the late '60s was Dennis Burns in his potent triple carb equipped Y block powered Model A bucket. In the top photo he is competing against regular opponent Denis Scully in his similarly motivated Model A bucket. Both cars were very low-slung.

VICTORIAN HOT ROD ASSOCIATION LIMITED

NATIONAL
DRAG RACING CHAMPIONSHIP

5th and 6th October, 1968

ENTRY FORM

This form must contain the following and be handed in at Classification— failure to comply will mean disqualification.

1. Weighbridge operator's signature.
2. Gate keeper's initials.
3. Classifier's classification and signature.

Official Use Only	Cubic Inches	Weight	Ratio	Class	Number
	272 C.I.	2150 lbs.		D/CR	24

USE BLOCK LETTERS (NO PENCIL)

ENTRANT OR SPONSOR OWNER — Name Dennis SCULLY — Tel. No. 37-1786 — Address 16 Riverview Rd. Essendon — Postcode 3040

DRIVER — Name as above — Address

BODY
Type of Body RDSTR — Interior YES
Body Modification YES
Year of Body 1928 — Make of Body FORD.
ENGINE
Year of Engine 1955 — Make of Engine FORD
Standard Bore YES — Over Bore — Cu. Ins. 272 — Exhaust HEADERS
Carburation TWO
GEAR BOX
Make of Box FORD — Year of Manufacture
DIFFERENTIAL
Ratio 3·63 — Year of Manufacture '52 Make OLDS
SUSPENSION
Stock — Altered YES — Make OWN
Wheelbase if altered 105°
Engine set back (No. 1 spark plug to front axle centre)
Engine Height (Crank pulley centre to ground)
Police Licence No. — AHRF No. (Licence)
Cams Licence No.

I hereby state that the above modifications and specifications are true and correct and that my car is subject to official impounding and re-classifying at any time during the Meeting.

Owner's Signature *D Scully*
Classifier's Signature

VICTORIAN HOT ROD ASSOCIATION LIMITED

NATIONAL DRAG RACING CHAMPIONSHIP

5th and 6th October, 1968

ENTRY FORM

This form must contain the following and be handed in at Classification— failure to comply will mean disqualification.

1. Weighbridge operator's signature.
2. Gate keeper's initials.
3. Classifier's classification and signature.

Official Use Only	Cubic Inches	Weight	Ratio	Class	Number
	283 C.I.	1120 lbs.		A/A	106

USE BLOCK LETTERS (NO PENCIL)

ENTRANT OR SPONSOR OWNER — Name STAN BAROUTSIS & ANDY BAROUTSIS — Tel. No.
Address 123 Thompson St — Postcode 3016
Name
Address Williamstown

DRIVER — Name
Address as above

BODY
Type of Body Fiat — Interior
Body Modification chop Top — Make of Body
Year of Body 1937
ENGINE
Year of Engine 1967 — Make of Engine Chev — Cu. Ins. 283
Standard Bore Stand — Over Bore 3 — Exhaust Headers
Carburation
GEAR BOX Ford
Make of Box — Year of Manufacture 1957
DIFFERENTIAL
Ratio 4.11 — Year of Manufacture 1957 Make Ford
SUSPENSION
Stock — Altered — Make
Wheelbase if altered — (No. 1 spark plug to front axle centre)
Engine set back
Engine Height — (Crank pulley centre to ground)
Police Licence No. 1412 11 — AHRF No. (Licence) 117 – 127
Cams Licence No.

I hereby state that the above modifications and specifications are true and correct and that my car is subject to official impounding and re-classifying at any time during the Meeting.

Owner's Signature
Classifier's Signature

VICTORIAN HOT ROD ASSOCIATION LIMITED

NATIONAL DRAG RACING CHAMPIONSHIP

5th and 6th October, 1968

ENTRY FORM

This form must contain the following and be handed in at Classification— failure to comply will mean disqualification.

1. Weighbridge operator's signature.
2. Gate keeper's initials.
3. Classifier's classification and signature.

Official Use Only	Cubic Inches	Weight	Ratio	Class	Number
	C.I.	1456 lbs.		E/MS	666

USE BLOCK LETTERS (NO PENCIL)

ENTRANT OR SPONSOR OWNER — Name KEN VIRGIN — Tel. No.
Address 33 Lucerne Grv Findon — Postcode SA 5023
Name KEN VIRGIN
Address As above

DRIVER — Name KEN VIRGIN
Address As above

BODY
Type of Body SEDAN — Interior
Body Modification CUSTOM BUMPER BARS — Make of Body V.W
Year of Body 1961
ENGINE
Year of Engine 1961 — Make of Engine V.W — Cu. Ins. 90.0
Standard Bore — Over Bore 83mm — Exhaust OWN
Carburation TWIN
GEAR BOX V.W
Make of Box — Year of Manufacture 1961
DIFFERENTIAL
Ratio STANDARD — Year of Manufacture 1961 Make V.W.
SUSPENSION
Stock — Altered No — Make V.W
Wheelbase if altered No — (No. 1 spark plug to front axle centre)
Engine set back No
Engine Height STANDARD — (Crank pulley centre to ground)
Police Licence No. 049035 — AHRF No. (Licence) 66
Cams Licence No. SL 38

I hereby state that the above modifications and specifications are true and correct and that my car is subject to official impounding and re-classifying at any time during the Meeting.

Owner's Signature
Classifier's Signature

TOP: Stan Baroutsis ran his Fiat Topolino "The Bug" in a couple of different forms, first as a coupe as shown at Castlereagh in red paint and later as a "roadster" as at the '68 Nationals at Calder Park.

ABOVE LEFT: Ken Virgin's VW raced out of Adelaide where this photo was taken at the SA Hot Rod & Custom Show.

ABOVE RIGHT: Before the days of inclusiveness Benny and Joe Gatt raced their "Aborigine" FX Holden out of Sydney, shown here against Satisfaction in race trim (see next page).

NATIONAL DRAG RACING CHAMPIONSHIP

5th and 6th October, 1968

ENTRY FORM

This form must contain the following and be handed in at Classification— failure to comply will mean disqualification.

1. Weighbridge operator's signature.
2. Gate keeper's initials.
3. Classifier's classification and signature.

Official Use Only	Cubic Inches	Weight	Ratio	Class	Number
	380 C.I.	2520 lbs.		A/GS	602

USE BLOCK LETTERS (NO PENCIL)

ENTRANT OR SPONSOR OWNER — Name FT DRAG TEAM — Tel. No.
Address as below
Name BEN GATT — Postcode 2165
Address 147 THE BOULEVARDE FAIRFEILD N.S.W.

DRIVER — Name BEN GATT
Address 147 THE BOULEVARDE FAIRFEILD

BODY
Type of Body H.D. SEDAN — Interior
Body Modification Nil
Year of Body — Make of Body HOLDEN
ENGINE
Year of Engine 1962 — Make of Engine FORD
Standard Bore No — Over Bore — Cu. Ins. 380
Carburation TWO FOUR BARR — Exhaust HEADERS
GEAR BOX
Make of Box FORD — Year of Manufacture 1962
DIFFERENTIAL
Ratio 3.78 — Year of Manufacture 1956 Make FORD
SUSPENSION
Stock YES — Altered NO — Make HOLDEN
Wheelbase if altered NO
Engine set back NO — (No. 1 spark plug to front axle centre)
Engine Height 20" — (Crank pulley centre to ground)
Police Licence No. 4925NH — AHRF No. (Licence)
Cams Licence No.

I hereby state that the above modifications and specifications are true and correct and that my car is subject to official impounding and re-classifying at any time during the Meeting.

Owner's Signature
Classifier's Signature

LEFT: A regular Top Eliminator winner of the period was Graham Withers in his Ampol fueller, shown here from the Rodsports '68 Nationals meeting report. The exerpt from the meeting program also makes interesting reading 50 years later. High winds and rough track surface played havoc with the fast cars at the Nationals.

AUSTRALIA'S TOP DRAG RACER

Graham Withers

Twenty-seven year old Melbourne driver Graham Withers, Australian champion 1966. Australian record holder, fastest man in Australia at 7.87 sec. 193 m.p.h. which was achieved at Surfers Paradise late last year.

Graham originally had a speed equipment business making floor shifts and is Australia's only professional drag racing driver. Married with two children, his wife's name is Lesley and she is a keen follower of motor sport and has driven the car herself.

Graham imported the chassis as a kit, built it in Australia, modified it to his own requirements, fitted a Hemi Chrysler putting out about 1,300 h.p.

He holds the strip record for all sanctioned hot rod strips in Australia. Whilst making a demonstration run recently he mistook the finish line and was unable to pull up in time, demolishing the chassis of the car. Luckily Graham only had minor injuries from which he is recovering. The motor, etc., were undamaged in the accident. Graham has rebuilt the chassis himself during the last fortnight and it will be driven at today's meeting by John Maher.

For the future Graham is selling this car, importing from America a new Ford single overhead cam 427 c.i. motor. Although not finalised it is likely that an American built chassis will also be imported for the motor. The motor will possibly give up to 1,500 h.p. and dragsters of this power range in America are recording under 7 sec. and up to 240 m.p.h.

Graham uses and recommends Ampol fuel and lubricants and it is interesting to note that the car is called the Ampol G.T. Rail and uses exactly the same type of oil available to you on any Ampol Service Station.

BELOW: The Pirotta Ford V8 powered FX Holden was a superstar amongst fans of early Holdens and was an entrant at the '68 Drag Championship. The FX is shown in full show trim here but was raced with different wheels and tyres (see previous page).

ABOVE: Alan and Ron Moore ran this potent FJ Holden at Castlereagh in NSW where they were consistent winners in the B/MP class. They also took the honours in that class at the '68 Nationals where this Rodsports photo was taken.

BELOW LEFT: Neil Kelly still drives his '35 Ford coupe on a regular basis, abeit after a couple of rebuilds, but it still looks essentially the same. He competed regularly in it way back in the sixties at Riverside, where this photo was taken and also at Calder Raceway, including the '68 Drag Racing Championships. Neil has been a member of the Melbourne suburban based Eagles Rod & Custom Club since the very early days.

BELOW: Another regular competitor amongst the early Holden racers was Barry Ferrari in his C/S class FJ Holden.

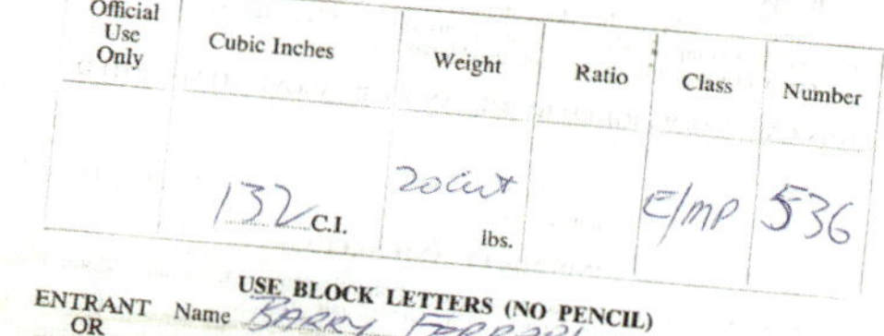

1968 NATIONALS

ABOVE & BELOW: Graham Rose ran his six cylinder dragster at most Riverside and Calder meets and he also entered a HK Monaro at the Nationals, but not the funny car version shown above, it came a little later.

BOTTOM: Over from South Australia was the Fiat Topolino altered of Ron Huchesson that ran Y block Ford power. Later Ron rebuilt the altered and updated the engine to a small block Ford Windsor.

ABOVE: Kevin Mayo raced this flathead powered dragster that also appeared often in hot rod shows as Kevin later became promoter of the VHRA Hot Rod Show in Victoria and was an active member of the Show Promoters Association.

RIGHT: Dyno Dave Bennett was very hard to beat at Calder in his almost brand new HK Holden 327 Monaro running in B/Stock class, shown here winning that class in a Rodsports Nationals report photo from 1968.

BELOW: Jim Robertson entered his C/Altered that featured a gutted '34 Ford coupe body. Jim ran this car at Riverside and continued with it at Calder for a short time after Riverside closed. It was Y block Ford powered.

BELOW: Another regular Sydney racer down for the Nationals at Calder was Bob Dunn in his big block 406 Ford powered T bucket altered.

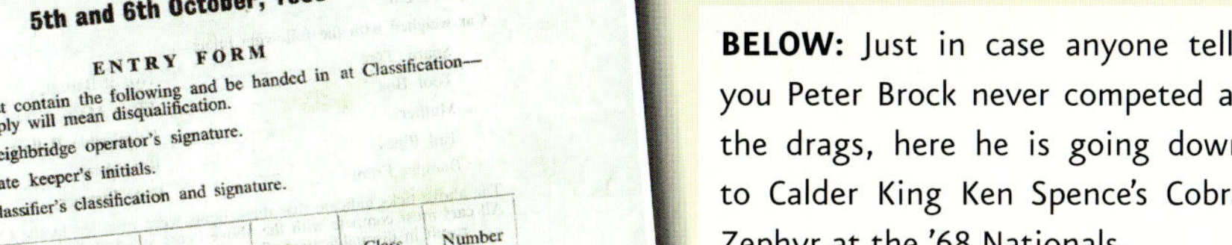

VICTORIAN HOT ROD ASSOCIATION LIMITED

NATIONAL DRAG RACING CHAMPIONSHIP

5th and 6th October, 1968

ENTRY FORM

This form must contain the following and be handed in at Classification—failure to comply will mean disqualification.

1. Weighbridge operator's signature.
2. Gate keeper's initials.
3. Classifier's classification and signature.

Official Use Only	Cubic Inches	Weight	Ratio	Class	Number
	406 C.I.	1624 lbs.		A/A	8P8.

USE BLOCK LETTERS (NO PENCIL)

ENTRANT OR SPONSOR OWNER — Name BOB DUNN — Tel. No. 72 3155
Address 13A CAMBRIDGE ST — Postcode 2166
Name BOB DUNN CANLEY HEIGHTS
Address 13A CAMBRIDGE ST CANLEY HEIGHTS

DRIVER — Name BOB DUNN
Address 13A CAMBRIDGE ST CANLEY HEIGHTS

BODY
Type of Body 23 T BUCKET — Interior —
Body Modification
Year of Body 1923 — Make of Body T FORD

ENGINE
Year of Engine 1963 — Make of Engine FORD GALAXIE
Standard Bore 4" — Over Bore 4⅛ — Cu. Ins. 406
Carburation 3 2 BARREL — Exhaust EXTRACTORS

GEAR BOX
Make of Box FAIRLANE — Year of Manufacture 1960

DIFFERENTIAL
Ratio 4.3:1 — Year of Manufacture 1940 — Make OLDSMOBILE.

SUSPENSION
Stock — Altered — Make HOME MADE.
Wheelbase if altered 100"
Engine set back 25% (No. 1 spark plug to front axle centre)
Engine Height 20 (Crank pulley centre to ground)
Police Licence No. 6497 SK — AHRF No. (Licence) 8P
Cams Licence No.

I hereby state that the above modifications and specifications are true and correct and that my car is subject to official impounding and re-classifying at any time during the Meeting.

Owner's Signature _______
Classifier's Signature _______

VICTORIAN HOT ROD ASSOCIATION LIMITED

NATIONAL DRAG RACING CHAMPIONSHIP

5th and 6th October, 1968

ENTRY FORM

This form must contain the following and be handed in at Classification—failure to comply will mean disqualification.

1. Weighbridge operator's signature.
2. Gate keeper's initials.
3. Classifier's classification and signature.

Official Use Only	Cubic Inches	Weight	Ratio	Class	Number
	179 C.I.	1680 lbs.		B/6	719

USE BLOCK LETTERS (NO PENCIL)

ENTRANT OR SPONSOR OWNER — Name DIAMOND VALLEY SPEED SHOP — Tel. No. 435 5585
Address 141 MAIN ST GREENSBOROUGH — Postcode 3088
Name AS ABOVE
Address

DRIVER — Name PETER BROCK
Address 141 MAIN ST GREENSBOROUGH

BODY
Type of Body AUSTIN A30 SEDAN — Interior
Body Modification — Make of Body AUSTIN A30
Year of Body 1953

ENGINE
Year of Engine 1965 — Make of Engine HOLDEN
Standard Bore YES — Over Bore — Cu. Ins. 179
Carburation 3 SU — Exhaust

GEAR BOX
Make of Box OPEL — Year of Manufacture 1967

DIFFERENTIAL
Ratio 3.89 — Year of Manufacture 1967 — Make HOLDEN

SUSPENSION
Stock NO — Altered YES — Make OWN
Wheelbase if altered NO
Engine set back YES (No. 1 spark plug to front axle centre)
Engine Height 13" (Crank pulley centre to ground)
Police Licence No. 157768 — AHRF No. (Licence)
Cams Licence No. V58

I hereby state that the above modifications and specifications are true and correct and that my car is subject to official impounding and re-classifying at any time during the Meeting.

Owner's Signature _______
Classifier's Signature _______

BELOW: Just in case anyone tells you Peter Brock never competed at the drags, here he is going down to Calder King Ken Spence's Cobra Zephyr at the '68 Nationals.

NATIONAL DRAG RACING CHAMPIONSHIP

5th and 6th October, 1968

ENTRY FORM

This form must contain the following and be handed in at Classification—failure to comply will mean disqualification.

1. Weighbridge operator's signature.
2. Gate keeper's initials.
3. Classifier's classification and signature.

Official Use Only	Cubic Inches	Weight	Ratio	Class	Number
	272 C.I.	2184 lbs.	B/6	B/CR	668

USE BLOCK LETTERS (NO PENCIL)

ENTRANT OR SPONSOR OWNER — Name LIDDELL IAN — Tel. No. 585213
Address 4 PORTLAND ST CARNEGIE — Postcode 3163
Name
Address SAME AS ABOVE

DRIVER — Name
Address

BODY
Type of Body BUCKET — Interior
Body Modification SHORTENED — Make of Body FORD
Year of Body 1928

ENGINE
Year of Engine 1956 — Make of Engine FORD
Standard Bore YES — Over Bore — Cu. Ins. 272 ci
Carburation STOCK — Exhaust

GEAR BOX
Make of Box FORD — Year of Manufacture 1939

DIFFERENTIAL
Ratio ? — Year of Manufacture — Make

SUSPENSION
Stock — Altered — Make
Wheelbase if altered
Engine set back (No. 1 spark plug to front axle centre)
Engine Height (Crank pulley centre to ground)
Police Licence No. — AHRF No. (Licence)
Cams Licence No.

I hereby state that the above modifications and specifications are true and correct and that my car is subject to official impounding and re-classifying at any time during the Meeting.

Owner's Signature Ian Liddell
Classifier's Signature _______

RIGHT: Ian Liddell raced his Model A bucket at the Calder Nationals having just moved down from Sydney at the time. The bucket was another Y block Ford powered car.

Australian National Drag RACING CHAMPIONSHIPS

Sunday, October 6th, 1968
CALDER DRAGWAY

Run in conjunction with the Vic. Hot Rod Association

Track Manager, Secretary of meeting	Jack Collins
Meeting Director	Bob Lees
Race Director	Norm Darwin
Classification	Mike Russo
Scrutineering	David Gale
Pit Marshal	Bob Dykes
Starting Marshal	Leo Spessot
Timing Technician	John Kidd
Timing Chief	Peter Fiddler
Announcers	Dick Munday — Start
	Keith Harvey — Finish
P.A. Co-ordinator	Roger Barrows
Recording	Heather Blair
Crowd Control	Jeff Hollingsworth

Crowd, pit, staging and other officials by members of V.H.R.A. recognised clubs.

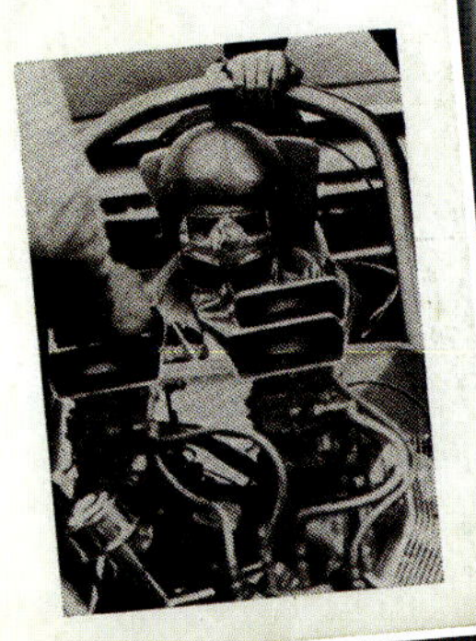

BELOW: Yes, this photo from the Rodsports '68 Nationals coverage is of a genuine Ford GT 40 participating at the Nationals. The car was owned at the time by Colin Hyams whose family owned the Melbourne Luna Park. He turned up at the drags at different times in several different, now very valuable cars. This GT 40 was originally sold to Colin Hyams in London and he drove it to various destinations in Europe before shipping it back to Australia. It was later sold to an Alan Copland in Australia and finished up back in the USA where it is now fully restored. In the background is Bob Jane's Elfin-Repco that was running high 12 second times at the Nationals.

The following entry form appears on the page:

VICTORIAN HOT ROD ASSOCIATION LIMITED

NATIONAL DRAG RACING CHAMPIONSHIP
5th and 6th October, 1968

ENTRY FORM

This form must contain the following and be handed in at Classification— failure to comply will mean disqualification.

1. Weighbridge operator's signature.
2. Gate keeper's initials.
3. Classifier's classification and signature.

Official Use Only	Cubic Inches	Weight	Ratio	Class	Number
	302 C.I.	2240 lbs.		A/SP	623

USE BLOCK LETTERS (NO PENCIL)

ENTRANT OR SPONSOR OWNER — Name: Colin Hyams — Tel. No. 244196 — Address: 6 Lansell Road — Postcode: — Name/Address: Toorak

DRIVER — Name/Address: As Above

BODY — Type of Body: GT Coupe — Interior: Stock — Body Modification: Nil — Make of Body: Ford — Year of Body: 1968

ENGINE — Year of Engine: 1968 — Make of Engine: Ford — Standard Bore: — Over Bore: — Cu. Ins.: 302 — Carburation: Webers — Exhaust: Stock

GEAR BOX — Make of Box: ZF — Year of Manufacture: 1968

DIFFERENTIAL — Ratio: Stock — Year of Manufacture: 1968 — Make: Ford

SUSPENSION — Stock: Stock — Altered: Stock — Make: — Wheelbase if altered: — Engine set back: (No. 1 spark plug to front axle centre) — Engine Height: (Crank pulley centre to ground) — Police Licence No.: — AHRF No. (Licence): — Cams Licence No.:

I hereby state that the above modifications and specifications are true and correct and that my car is subject to official impounding and re-classifying at any time during the Meeting.

Owner's Signature: [signature]

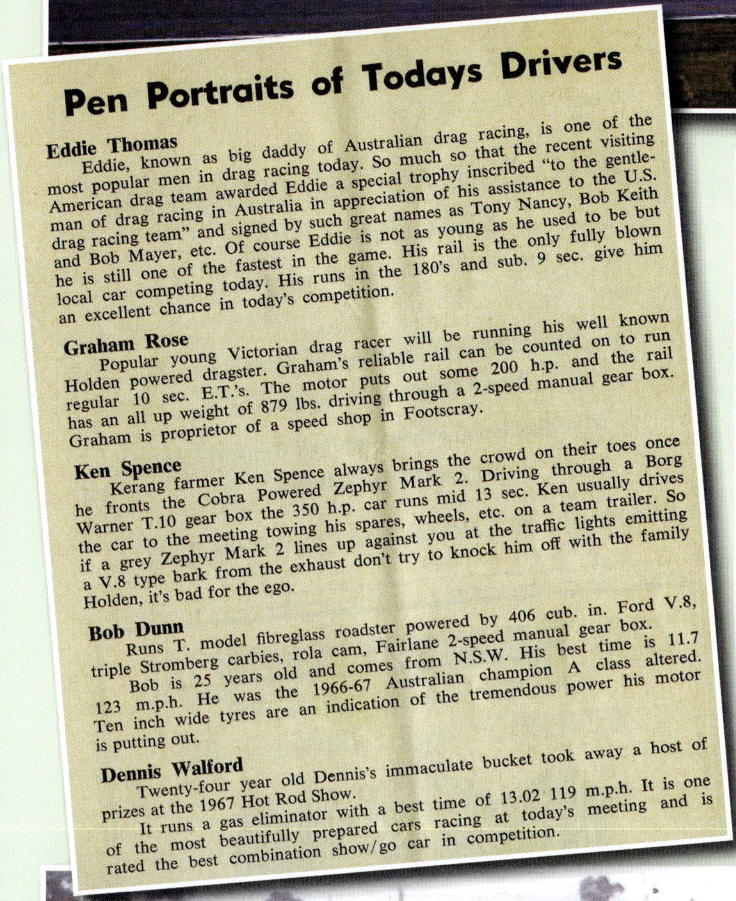

Pen Portraits of Todays Drivers

Eddie Thomas

Eddie, known as big daddy of Australian drag racing, is one of the most popular men in drag racing today. So much so that the recent visiting American drag team awarded Eddie a special trophy inscribed "to the gentleman of drag racing in Australia in appreciation of his assistance to the U.S. drag racing team" and signed by such great names as Tony Nancy, Bob Keith and Bob Mayer, etc. Of course Eddie is not as young as he used to be but he is still one of the fastest in the game. His rail is the only fully blown local car competing today. His runs in the 180's and sub. 9 sec. give him an excellent chance in today's competition.

Graham Rose

Popular young Victorian drag racer will be running his well known Holden powered dragster. Graham's reliable rail can be counted on to run regular 10 sec. E.T.'s. The motor puts out some 200 h.p. and the rail has an all up weight of 879 lbs. driving through a 2-speed manual gear box. Graham is proprietor of a speed shop in Footscray.

Ken Spence

Kerang farmer Ken Spence always brings the crowd on their toes once he fronts the Cobra Powered Zephyr Mark 2. Driving through a Borg Warner T.10 gear box the 350 h.p. car runs mid 13 sec. Ken usually drives the car to the meeting towing his spares, wheels, etc. on a team trailer. So if a grey Zephyr Mark 2 lines up against you at the traffic lights emitting a V.8 type bark from the exhaust don't try to knock him off with the family Holden, it's bad for the ego.

Bob Dunn

Runs T. model fibreglass roadster powered by 406 cub. in. Ford V.8, triple Stromberg carbies, rola cam, Fairlane 2-speed manual gear box. Bob is 25 years old and comes from N.S.W. His best time is 11.7 123 m.p.h. He was the 1966-67 Australian champion A class altered. Ten inch wide tyres are an indication of the tremendous power his motor is putting out.

Dennis Walford

Twenty-four year old Dennis's immaculate bucket took away a host of prizes at the 1967 Hot Rod Show.

It runs a gas eliminator with a best time of 13.02 119 m.p.h. It is one of the most beautifully prepared cars racing at today's meeting and is rated the best combination show/go car in competition.

FAR LEFT: Here's the official program from the 1968 Australian National Drag Racing Campionships at Calder Raceway. Check out the list of officials and you will recognise many familiar names from early Australian Hot Rodding and drag racing days. The Track Manager was none other than Jack "Fizzball" Collins who won the Top Eliminator prize at the very first Australian Drag Racing National Championships at Fishermans Bend (Riverside) in 1965. Pit Marshall Bob Dykes went on to become the long-term chief of the Australian Street Rod Federation and many of the other names on this list are still active in the car scene today.

LEFT: Pen portraits of some of the top competitors at the Nationals were included in the program as well. All are familiar names to anyone who followed the world of drag racing and hot rodding in Australia at the time.

ABOVE: The subject of one of those pen portraits was Ken Spence, seen in action here in his potent 289 Cobra powered Zephyr against a GT Falcon. Ken was King of the Hill at Calder and regularly match raced other high profile competitors to round out an otherwise early finishing race day.

BELOW: There were always street rods parked in the front row of the parking lot at Calder Raceway during this period. In the background of this photo is Eddie Ford's Y block powered green '34 Ford coupe, next to the motorcycle is a small block Ford V8 powered Austin Healey that was owned by Merve Williams and the '34 Ford coupe in the foreground was owned at the time by Graham South.

BELOW: At the head of this line outside the Castlemaine Visitor Centre is Luke Furlong's blue XP Falcon sedan, next is Corey Wilson's Model A and his mother Jeanette's '48 Ford coupe with '42 front sheetmetal.

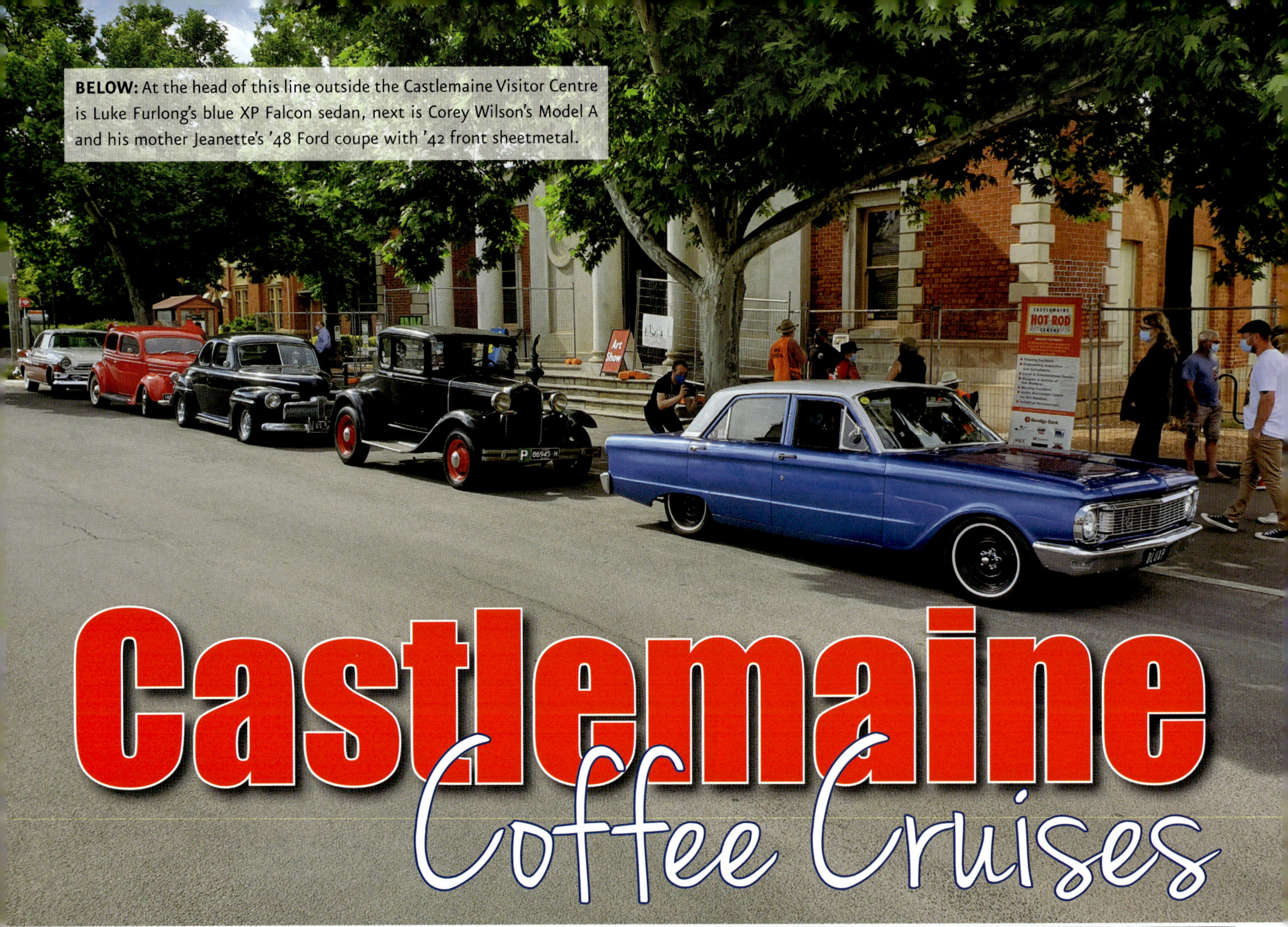

Castlemaine Coffee Cruises

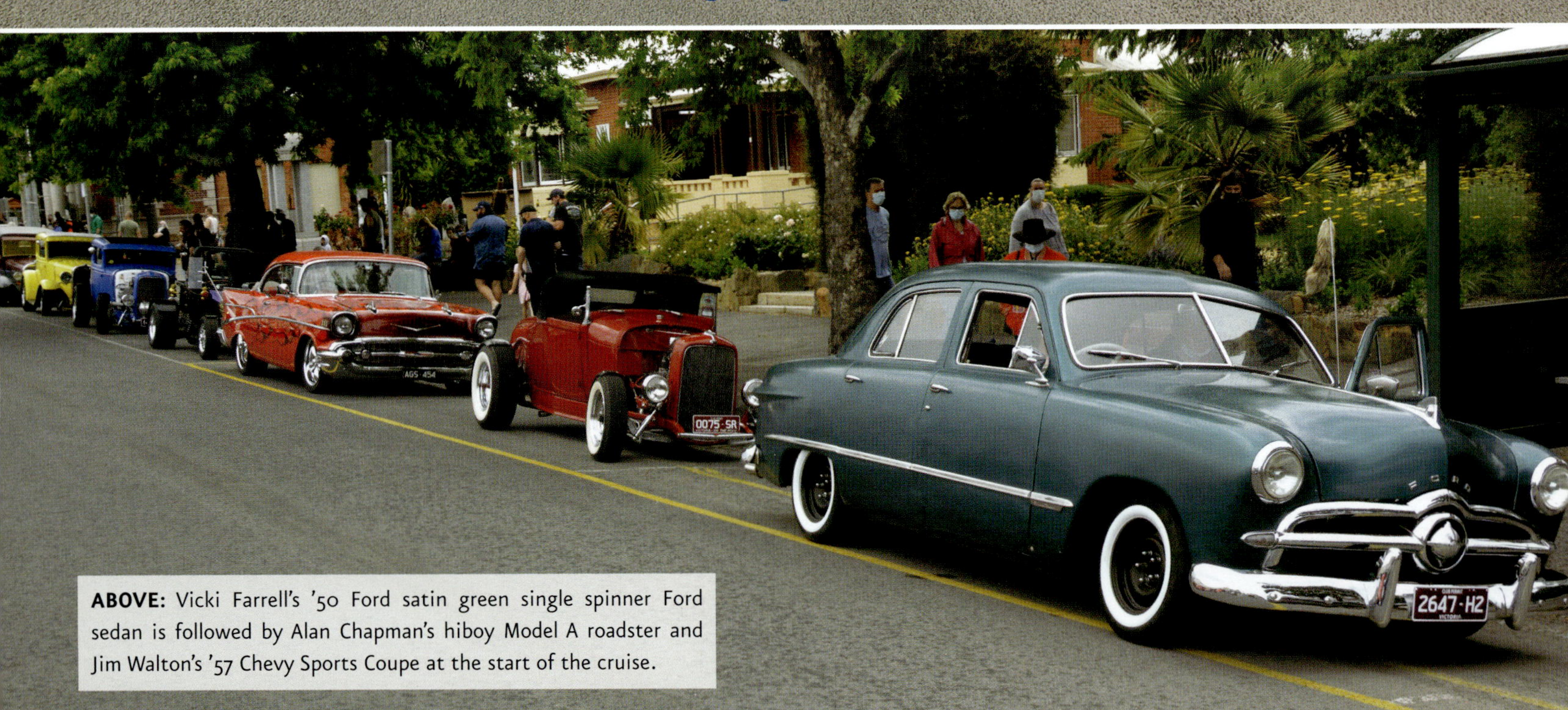

ABOVE: Vicki Farrell's '50 Ford satin green single spinner Ford sedan is followed by Alan Chapman's hiboy Model A roadster and Jim Walton's '57 Chevy Sports Coupe at the start of the cruise.

The COVID-19 pandemic put a stop to automotive events almost right around the world, but the pandemic hasn't been quite as bad in the Southern Hemisphere, particularly in places like Australia and New Zealand. By November 2020 it was clear that Australia was coming out of the pandemic to such an extent that some events could start forward planning again. Easily organised attractions like coffee cruises were first to resume and in our own local area the Castlemaine Hot Rod Centre cruises were amongst the first. Here's a snapshot of activity from the first three cruises heading into 2021. ■

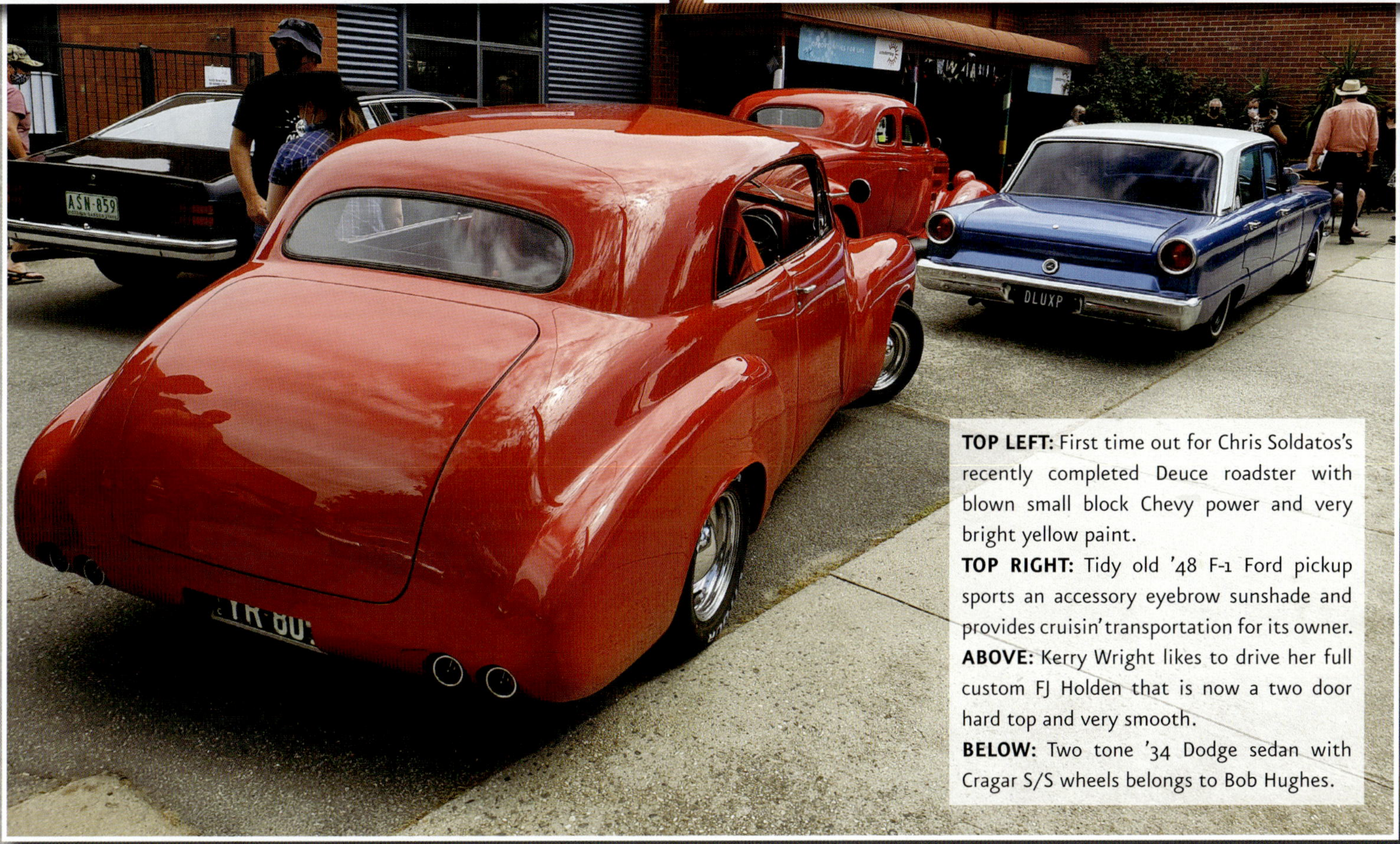

TOP LEFT: First time out for Chris Soldatos's recently completed Deuce roadster with blown small block Chevy power and very bright yellow paint.

TOP RIGHT: Tidy old '48 F-1 Ford pickup sports an accessory eyebrow sunshade and provides cruisin' transportation for its owner.

ABOVE: Kerry Wright likes to drive her full custom FJ Holden that is now a two door hard top and very smooth.

BELOW: Two tone '34 Dodge sedan with Cragar S/S wheels belongs to Bob Hughes.

ABOVE: Nicely proportioned '31 Model A coupe on Deuce rails and stuffed full of Hemi driveline is owned by Jeff Gartside of Harcourt.

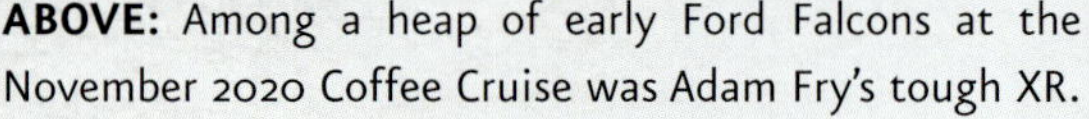

ABOVE: Among a heap of early Ford Falcons at the November 2020 Coffee Cruise was Adam Fry's tough XR.

BELOW: Nice old Desoto coupe is the pride and joy of Craig Thomas, a regular on the Castlemaine Cruises.

ABOVE: Now moving into the age of classics are the early Commodores like this VL model owned by Glenn Wybar. Low profile tyres on gold spoked wheels give it street cred.

ABOVE LEFT: Black late model Mustang is a welcome participant because the only criteria for joining in is to bring a car you love.

ABOVE: Early Mustangs are more popular than ever, especially considering they weren't sold new in any large numbers in Australia.

ABOVE: Mark Thomas' Ford Falcon Deluxe has billet style wheels but retains original six cylinder running gear. Son, Logan loves to go on the Coffee Cruises with dad.

ABOVE: Rick Williams' gold Torana is an LJ model that retains its original Holden six powerplant and rolls on a set of widened steel wheels. These Toranas were based on an English Vauxhall body with longer nose for the six.

ABOVE: Richard Caddy keeps this XY Falcon GT in immaculate condition. It has been a Castlemaine area vehicle since new.

ABOVE RIGHT: White Corvette is new to Castlemaine and was entered by local enthusiast Craig Hoskin.

RIGHT: Another XY Falcon GT, this time the Electric Blue example of Brad Sturgess.

BELOW: Greg Hadfield has been a Mustang collector since he was a boy. This is his immaculate '65 coupe.

Castlemaine
Coffee Cruises

LEFT: Looking like a period race car is the hiboy '32 Ford roadster of Rod Hadfield parked with Bruce Helms' flat black '50 Studebaker two door.

MAIN: Victorian ASRF Rep Bruce Helms' 1950 Studebaker, Peter and Helen Edwards' maroon '68 C3 Chevy Corvette roadster, Lenny Wood's pale green '67 Mustang coupe, Jim and Elaine Walton's flamed '57 Chev hardtop.

BELOW: Two door Studebaker Commander of Anita and Ash Cronin leads this group through the Harcourt roundabout on the way to Mount Alexander.

ABOVE: Local Mustang enthusiast Vin Cappy attended in his '66 coupe that remains stock right down to its original wheel caps.

www.graffitipub.com.au

RIGHT: Rick Townsend's V8 XA Falcon coupe is a regular cruiser.
BELOW: Ballarat Road Rodders club member, Chris Kelly owns this old beast. The big sedan is a 1947 Nash equipped with HQ Holden V8 running gear.

ABOVE: Even a basic XY Falcon sedan makes a great coffee cruiser and is a real classic now that it is over 50 years old!

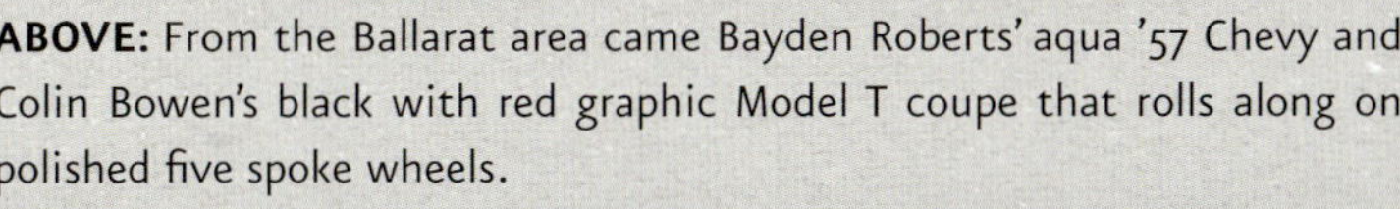

ABOVE: From the Ballarat area came Bayden Roberts' aqua '57 Chevy and Colin Bowen's black with red graphic Model T coupe that rolls along on polished five spoke wheels.

ABOVE: Classic American rocket era styling doesn't get more elaborate than the '59 Plymouth Belvedere. This nice example has quite a history and is owned by Greg Carr of Elphinstone, Vic.

Castlemaine
Coffee Cruises

RIGHT: Patina paint with faded signs makes Brendan Winwood's Chevy pickup look as if it has been around in this form for years.

BELOW: Another local car with a long history is the '48 Ford coupe of Jeanette Wilson. It has worn '42 Ford front sheetmetal for some time and was previously owned by several high profile Victorian rodders.

ABOVE: Paul Turkentine and his partner, Maggie recently moved to Castlemaine from the Canberra area and brought their tidy T bucket out for the cruise. This car was featured in ASR 172.

ABOVE RIGHT: A number of cars travelled over from Ballarat on their own cruise and met up with us at Cream Town cafe, including Andrew Hodges in his '34 Tudor.

RIGHT: Larry O'Toole's 396 Chevy powered '28 Model A Tudor has been on the road for over 45 years and still going strong.

ABOVE: At the head of this group at the Big Hill Winery is Ross Harding's cream with flames '30 Model A Ford roadster ute. Next is Ian Bentley's green '30 Model A coupe with chrome wheels and flathead power.

LEFT: Blue Dodge Charger is a choice muscle car once owned by Tex Smith and now owned by Matthew Chapman.

BELOW: A regular participant at the Castlemaine Coffee Cruises is Rob Louden in his yellow '30 Model A Ford coupe.

LEFT: This 1931 Model A Ford coupe was built back in the eighties by Ian Nye and won Top Street Rod at the 1985 ASRF Street Rod Nationals at Canberra. It now belongs to Adrian Lohse.

BELOW LEFT: Juie and Mick Loomes own both of these Model A sedans. The chopped red hot rod was built in Queensland many years ago by the late Darryl Kuhnemann.

BELOW: Al Chapman navigating a windy road in his flatty powered Model A Ford roadster.

BOTTOM: Another flathead V8 powered Model A coupe. This one was recently completed by Ian Bentley from Bendigo.

ABOVE: This 1967 Ford Galaxie 500 convertible is the perfect family cruiser for this type of event. It belongs to Karl Brohan.

ABOVE RIGHT: The red home-built Deuce roadster of Kelly Boyle travelled from Ballarat.

RIGHT: Ken James from Harcourt cruising his '56 Chevy sedan.

BOTTOM: Parked up at the Big Hill Winery we have Marcus Elderfield's satin maroon '28 Model A Ford sedan delivery alongside Bubby Swift's Aussie bodied '33 Ford five window coupe and Noel Inman's '22 Centre Door Model T sedan.

ABOVE: Jason Borg's imported two door Fairlane and an Aussie bodied '36 Chevy sloper.

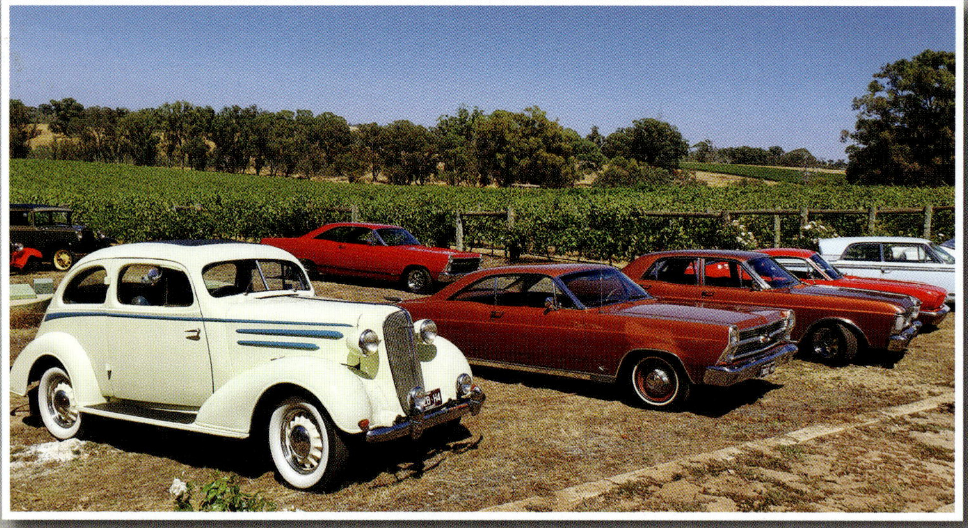

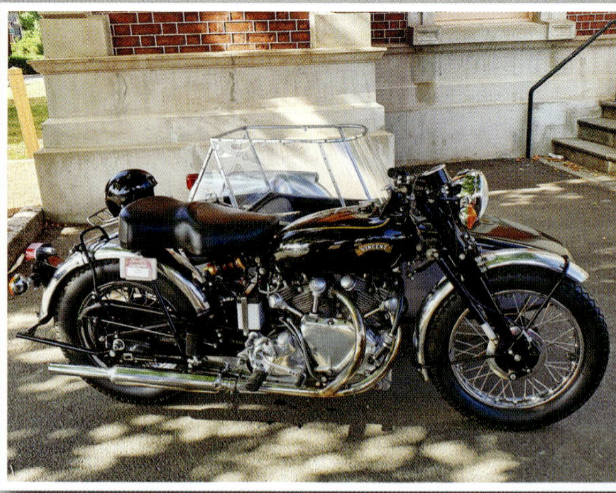

ABOVE: Want to turn hot rodders heads with your motorcycle outfit? Roll in with your desirable Vincent like Adam Pratt did.

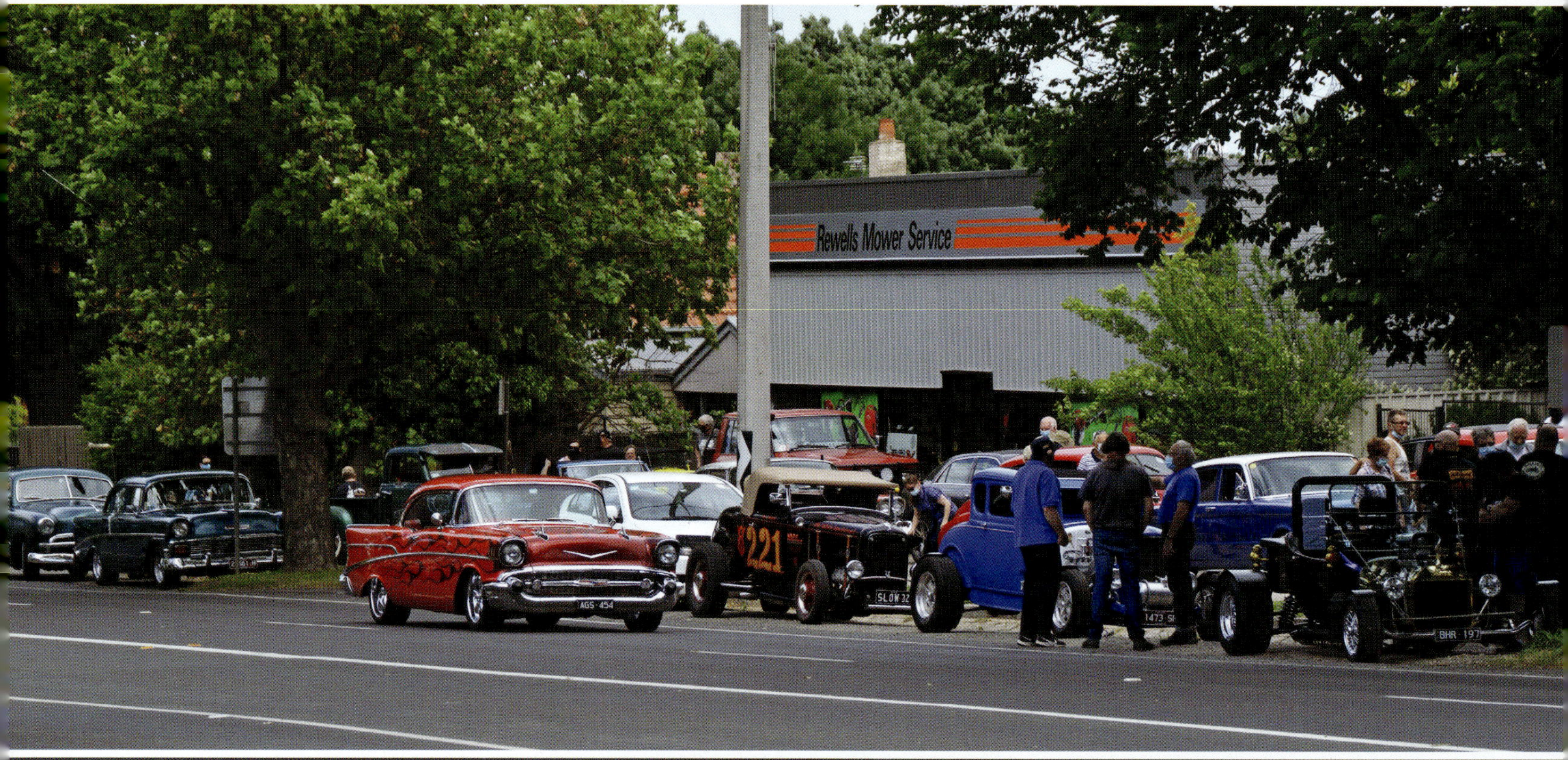

RIGHT: Northern Suburbs Street Rods member, Ray McDonald travelled up from Melbourne in his '39 Ford. **BELOW:** Ken and Rosalie Poynton's rare 1941 Pontiac roadster ute parked at the Big Hill Winery.

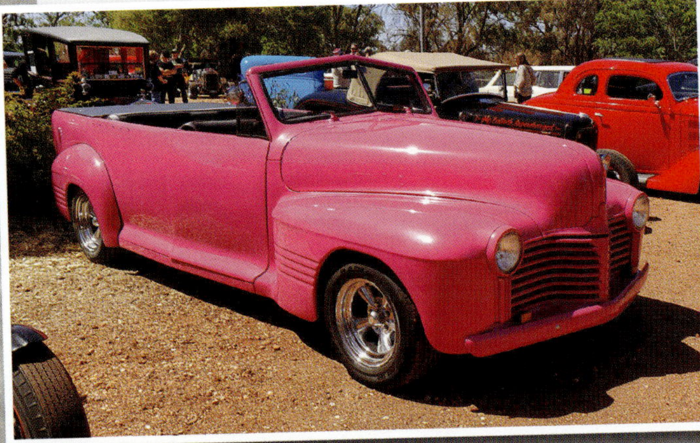

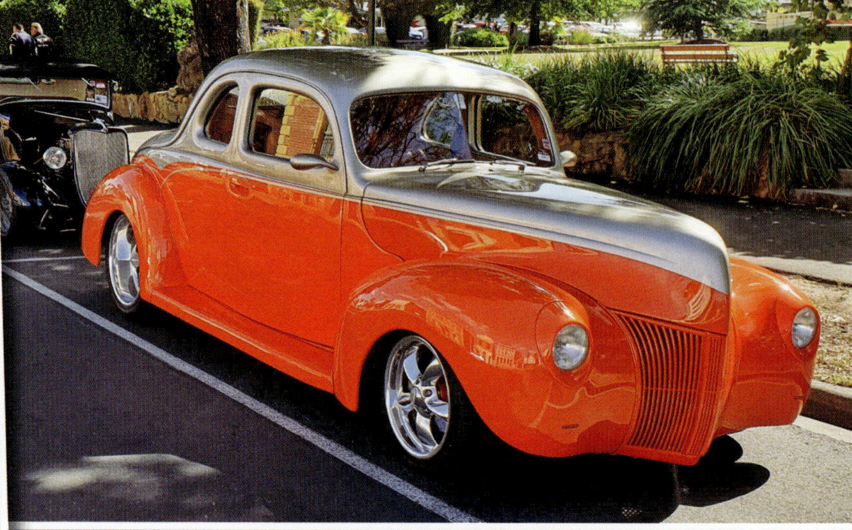

ABOVE: The winding Golden Point Road through the hills between Faraday and Chewton provided a neat spot for photos as the cruisers slowed down and bunched up together. This bright yellow Deuce roadster is the latest from Castlemaine drag racer and hot rodder, Chris Soldatos.

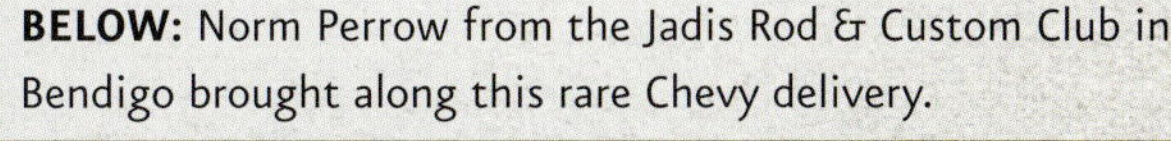
BELOW: Norm Perrow from the Jadis Rod & Custom Club in Bendigo brought along this rare Chevy delivery.

BELOW: Glenn Britten drove his HJ Holden station wagon over from Maryborough.

ABOVE: Chad Silvey travelled over with the Ballarat crew in his slammed on the deck 1965 Chevy pickup.

ABOVE: Superbly restored EH Holden sedan is a real collector's item these days. This one is owned by Shirley Elderfield.

ABOVE: Note the extreme differences between the cream coloured stock FJ Holden on the left and Kerry Wright's heavily customised two door hardtop. Other cars in this lineup include Jason White's yellow Model A Ford roadster, Jeff Gartside's Hemi powered A coupe and Geoff Knape's Holden V8 motivated '34 Ford Tudor.
LEFT: This 390 FE powered 1963 Ford Galaxie 500 XL hardtop looks great rolling along on solid Center Line rims.

Castlemaine Coffee Cruises

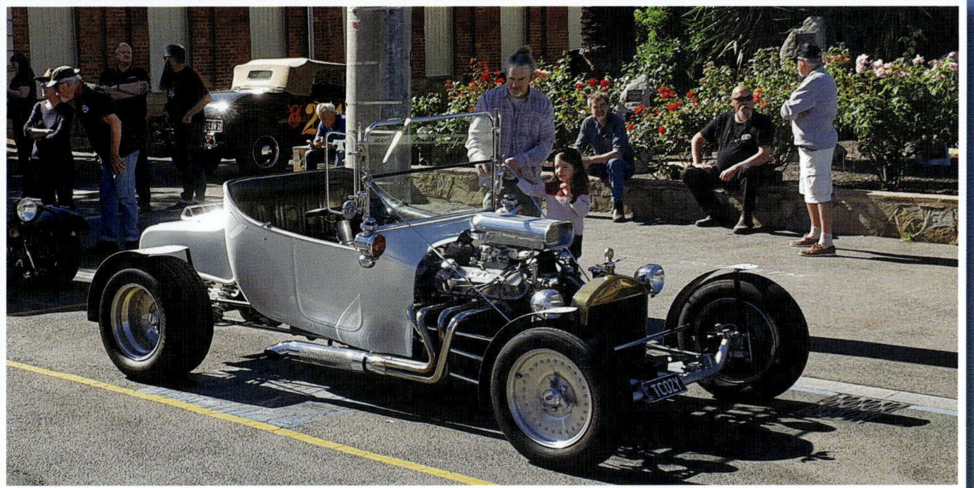

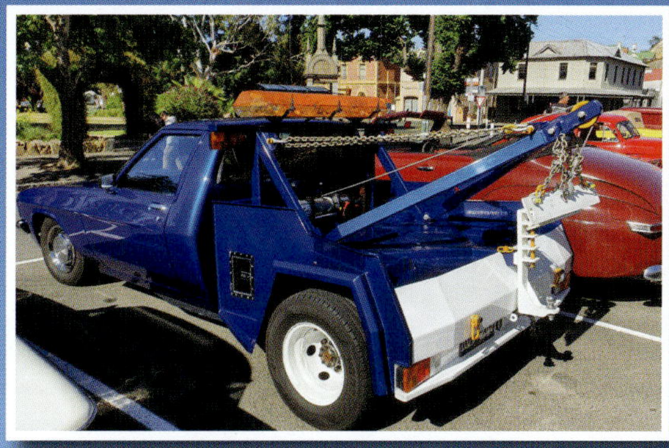

ABOVE: Rick's Ling's '23 T turtledeck was built in the late seventies by Keiran Otto using the first McDonald Bros kit ever sold.
ABOVE RIGHT: Neat Holden one tonner ute converted to a tow truck is a real head turner. It's often seen cruising around Castlemaine.

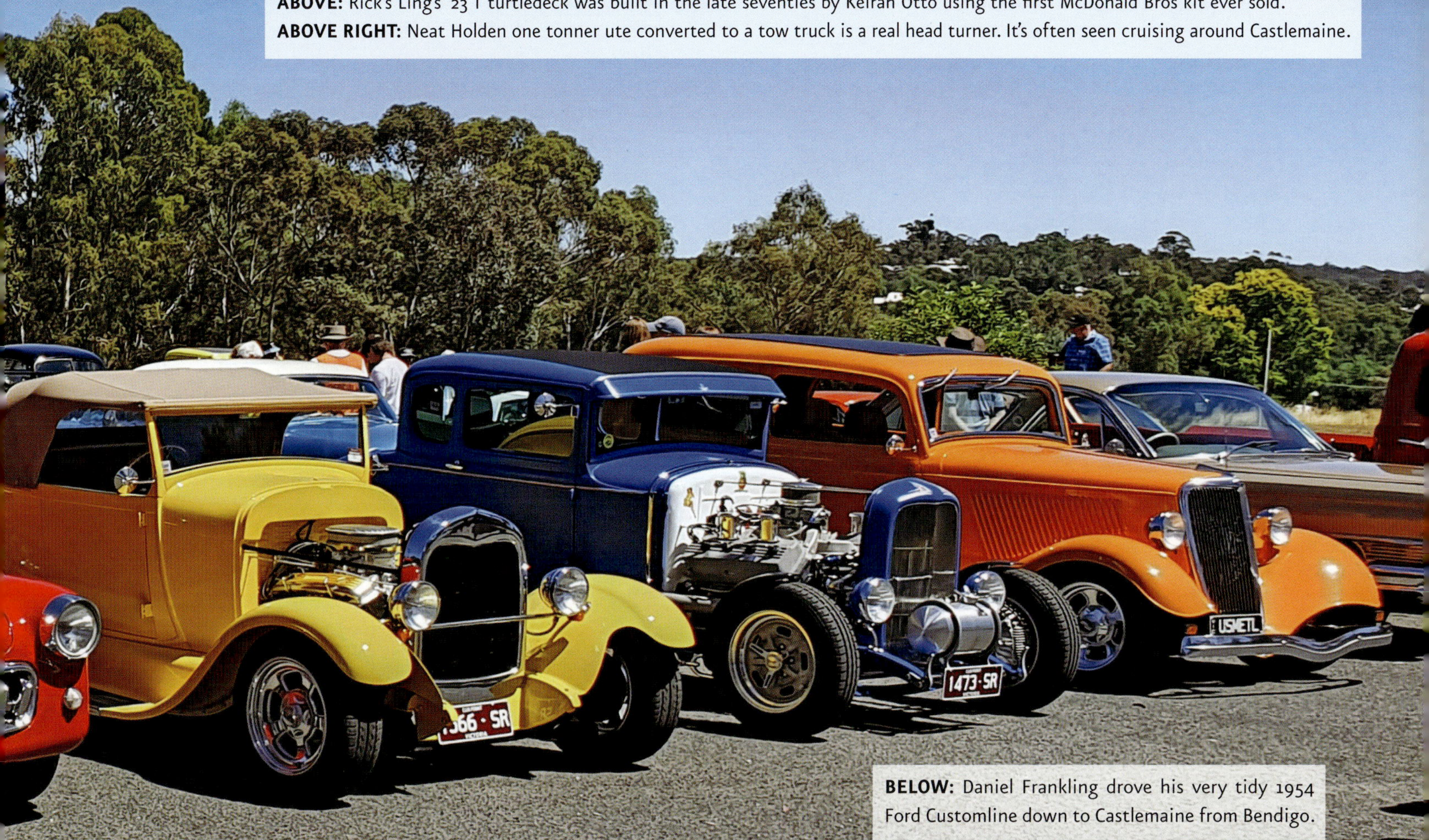

BELOW: Daniel Frankling drove his very tidy 1954 Ford Customline down to Castlemaine from Bendigo.

BELOW: Another local rodder that rolls up with a different car for each cruise is Rod Henderson. This time he had his '33 Ford Tudor out for the day.

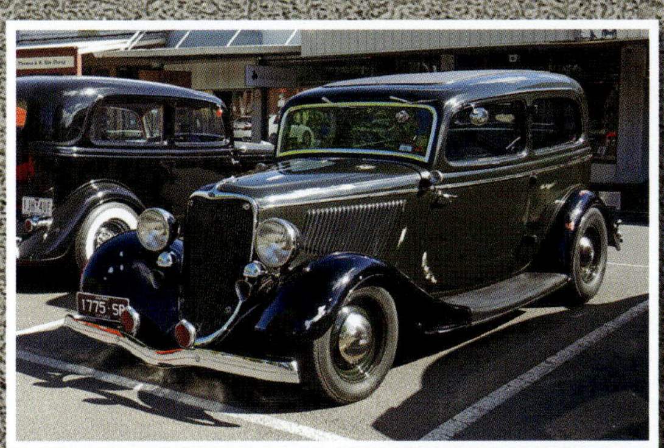

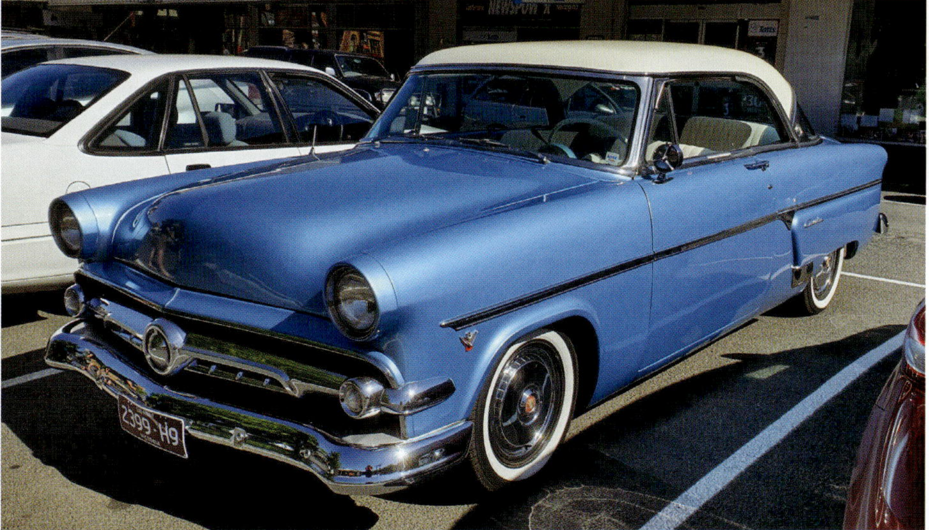

RIGHT: Lindsay Gunston's Deuce coupe sports red interior trim and runs a small block Chevy V8 topped with four two barrel carbies.
BELOW: Two red roadsters, the '33 on the left was built by the late Harry Wright and now belongs to George and Chris Windus of Bendigo while the '34 was constructed by local hot rodder, Geoff Knape.
BELOW LEFT: Another local, Con Soldatos owns this wild '36 Ford coupe. Con transformed this car from drag racing beast to street cruiser but it still uses a full tube race chassis and blown big block Chev.
BELOW RIGHT: This neat El Camino belongs to Jason Whatley.
BOTTOM: Black 1940 Ford coupe is a fine example of the breed. This one belongs to Don Hammond from Diggers Rest.

Castlemaine Coffee Cruises

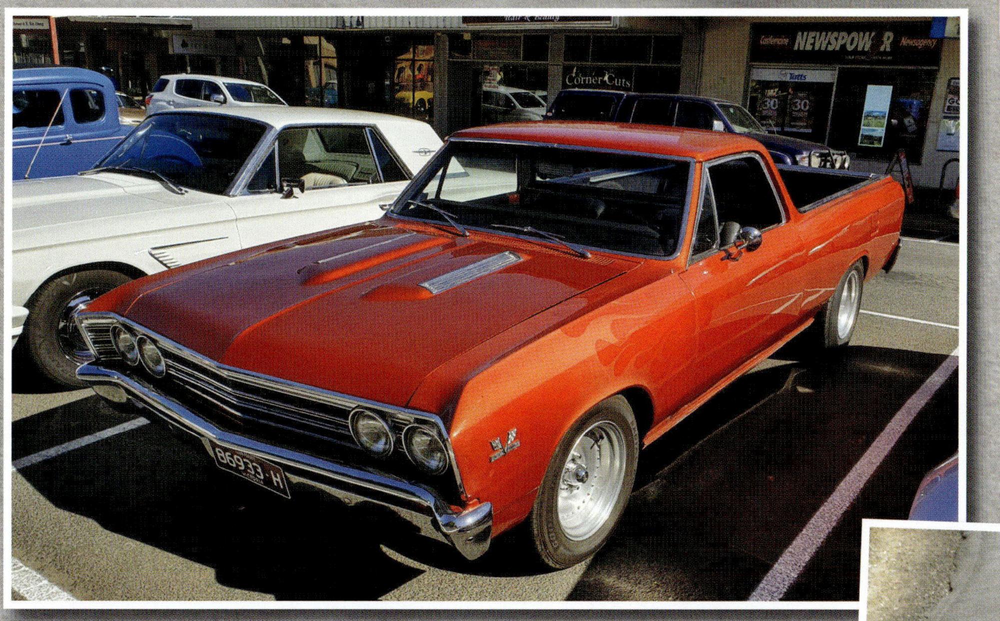

LEFT: Another cool El Camino seen at Castlemaine Coffee Cruises is this bronze example. It belongs to Mick Kimpton from Bendigo.

BELOW LEFT: This big Pontiac hardtop sedan looks tough with its raised white letter tyres, Boyd Coddington wheels and grey paintwork.

BELOW: Castlemaine Rods member, Mark Hadfield's '33 Ford sedan has been on the road for many years. It's chopped two inches and runs a 454 big block Chevy backed by a Turbo 400 and S Type Jaguar rear end. The car has never been unregistered from new.

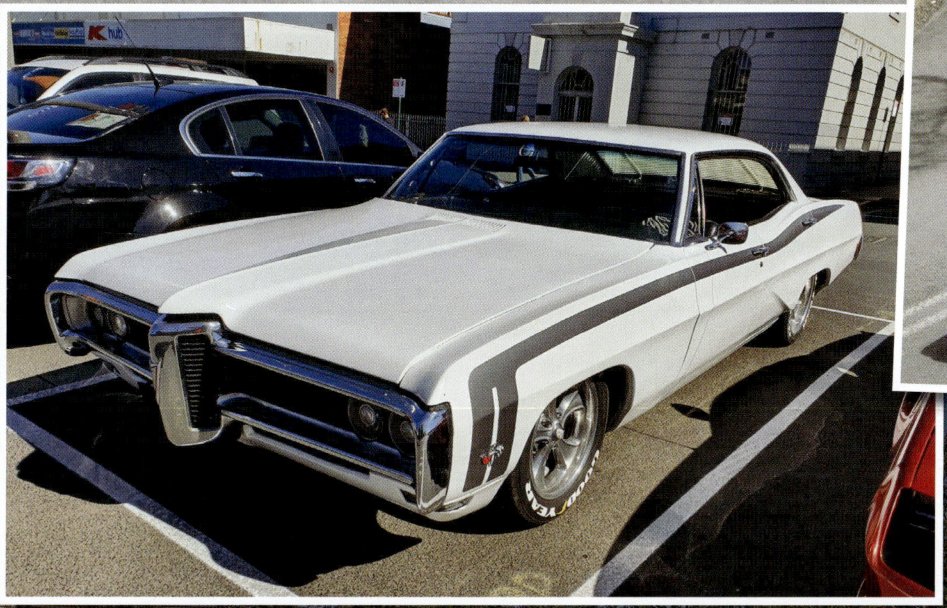

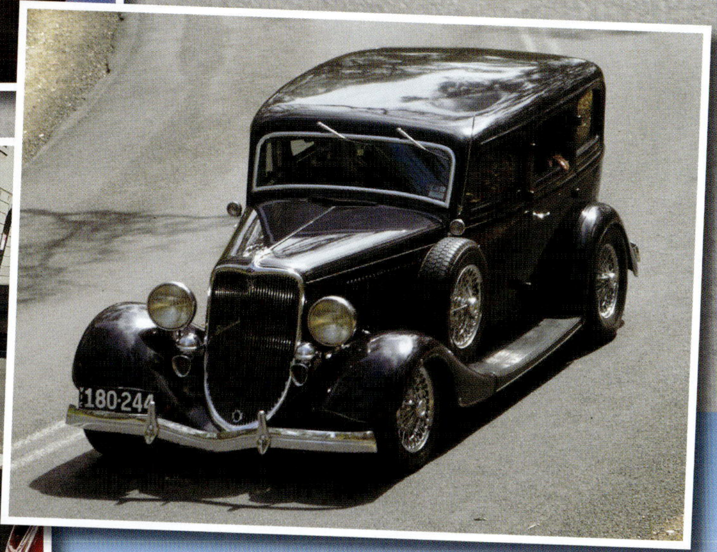

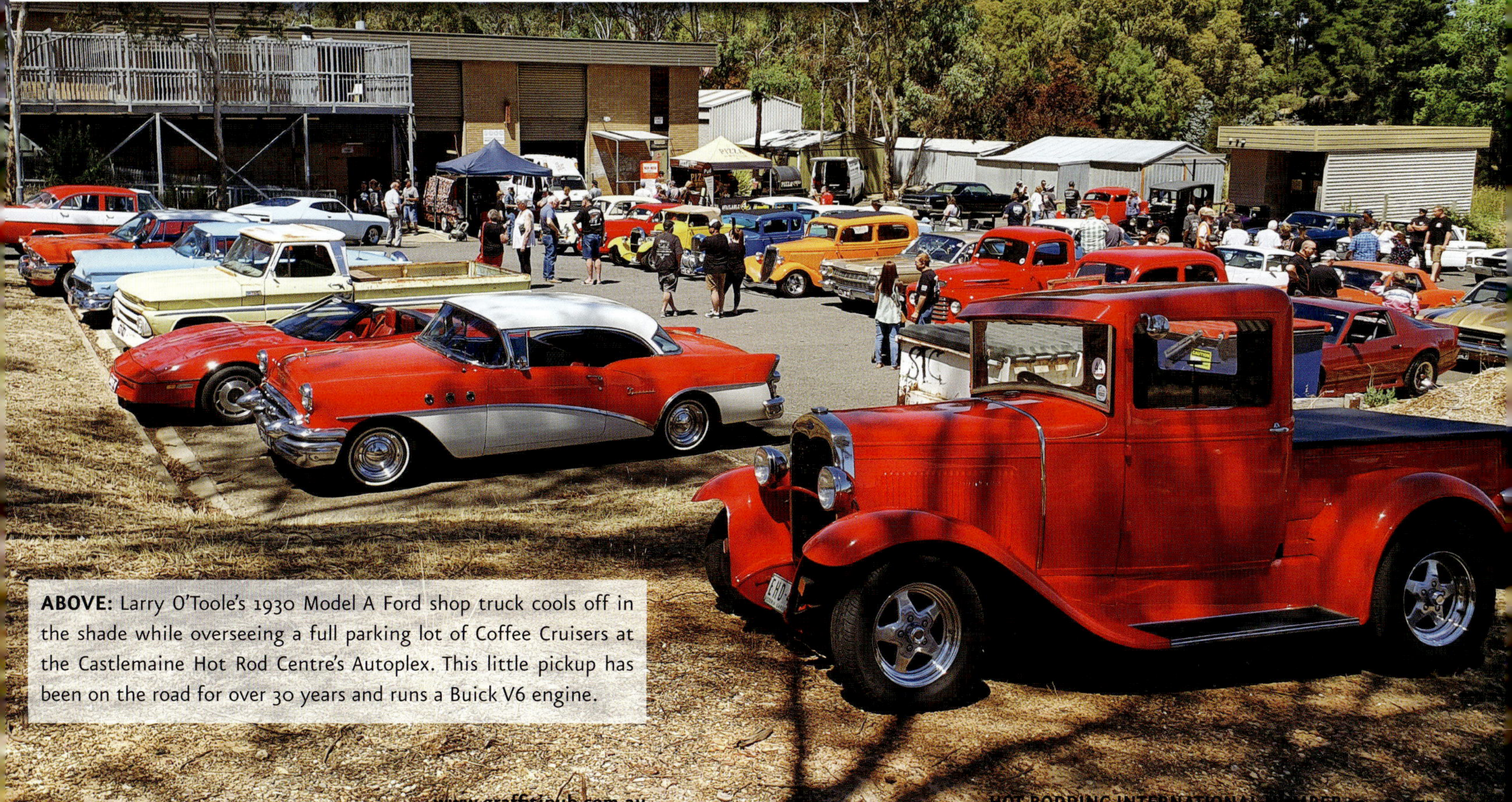

ABOVE: Larry O'Toole's 1930 Model A Ford shop truck cools off in the shade while overseeing a full parking lot of Coffee Cruisers at the Castlemaine Hot Rod Centre's Autoplex. This little pickup has been on the road for over 30 years and runs a Buick V6 engine.

T Bucket Renaissance
There's life in the old fad car yet!

ABOVE: Perfect stance and wheel tyre combination makes John Davis and Tracy Schmidt's black T bucket an outstanding example that belies its original early 1970s build date. Add in a big block Ford engine, lots of polished and chromed metal, a perfectly fitted top, brass radiator, headlights and cowl lights, plus white interior trim and you have the complete package. Oh, there's a good looking Jag rear end twirling away under the rear too.

INSET ABOVE: Another survivor from the 1970s is Malcolm Mountjoy's yellow and green T that he won as first prize in an Australian Street Rod Federation raffle in 1977 and has kept in pristine condition ever since. Originally built in South Australia in the early 1970s by Trevor Eccles, this bucket has Y block Ford engine, typical roll topped black interior trim and chromed outside the rail headers. Not a bad investment for the princely sum of $5.00!

T Bucket Renaissance

LEFT: Here's an overhead view of Pete Swift's black T bucket shown on the previous spread. From this angle you can clearly see the buttoned red interior trim, so typical of sixties hot rods. Swifty based his T on a similar one he saw in an early Hot Rod magazine and his bucket has become a significant survivor in the Australian hot rodding scene. The round tanks suits perfectly.

BELOW: Most T buckets are built from readily available commercial kits, but they all end up looking different, thanks to the individuality of hot rodders all over the world. This orange California version displays hints of recent construction through the use of chopped down, slanted windshield and contemporary billet wheels. Engine is tunnel ram equipped small block Chevy.

ABOVE: Taken at the NSRA Nationals in Louisville, KY, this green T is a simple kit-based item from BeBops Glassworks. Note the popular aircraft style alloy seats, white painted suspension, steel wheels and simple styling. Building your own T bucket from a kit like this is an easy way to get into the hobby.

BELOW LEFT & RIGHT: Nothing says "Hot Rod" quite like a well proportioned T bucket like this one owned by Robert Hulog. Note the opposed spring front suspension, blown Chevy engine with straight, full length headers, low-cut body and perfectly proportioned top. A polished Jag rear end under such a T is almost compulsory. Can you tell that Jim Babb, Roger Jacobs and Dan Woods all had a hand in it?

TOP: It might have a turtle deck rear but there is no doubt Brett Martin's candy red T is still a bucket. It's another Australian survivor from the 1970s, originally built by Stan Kaminskis with blown small block Ford power and now fitted with polished Center Line wheels.

ABOVE: Yet another different style for a T bucket is the narrow bodied look of an early lakes modified, but built for the street with twin carb equipped flathead Ford engine and white Kelsey Hayes wire wheels. This one uses a cut down and widened Deuce grille shell out front.

ABOVE: Graeme Williams built his T bucket 50 years ago, sold it and later bought it back and restored it to its original configuration with blown Chevy engine, spoked alloy front wheels and buttoned white interior trim. It appeared on the cover of the first issue of Australian Street Rodding magazine, again on the cover of the 40th anniversary edition and recently completed a long overseas trip from Australia to the USA to take part in the 50th NSRA Street Rod Nationals. That's dedication!

BELOW: There can only be one name for a blown big block Chevy powered T bucket – "Nastee". This beast has been on the Australian scene for many years and still looks as good as the day it was finished.

T Bucket Renaissance

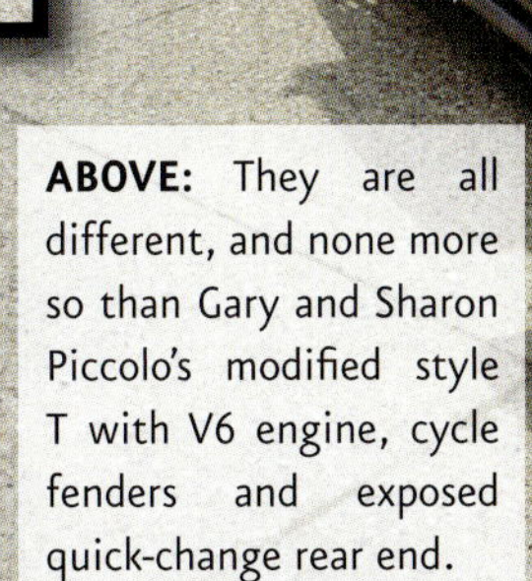

ABOVE: They are all different, and none more so than Gary and Sharon Piccolo's modified style T with V6 engine, cycle fenders and exposed quick-change rear end.

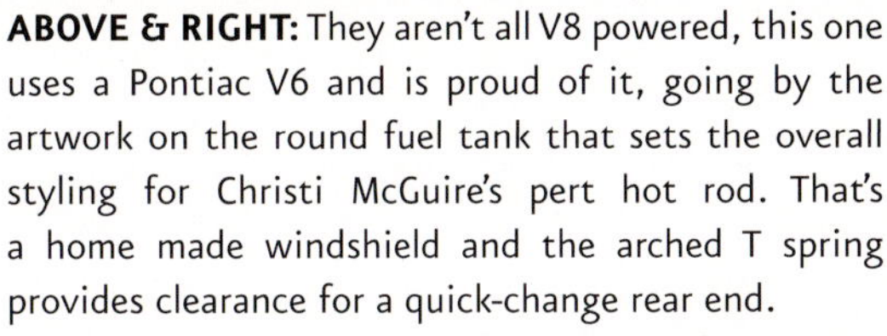

ABOVE & RIGHT: They aren't all V8 powered, this one uses a Pontiac V6 and is proud of it, going by the artwork on the round fuel tank that sets the overall styling for Christi McGuire's pert hot rod. That's a home made windshield and the arched T spring provides clearance for a quick-change rear end.

BELOW: Skinny wire wheels are typical American styling for T buckets that would struggle for legal compliance anywhere else. This bucket combines pale lemon body colour with beige top to achieve a level of sophistication in styling. Jerry Moody opted for a small block Ford engine to power his T to the Goodguys West Coast Nationals in Pleasanton, CA.

ABOVE: Rod Hadfield owns a stable of street rods that include this satin black turtledeck T that uses a Chrysler Hemi engine and genuine wide Halibrand rear wheels combined with original Model A items on the front.

ABOVE: Russell Hicks built the Mini 7 for his toddler son Robert back in the early sevemties using the running gear from an Austin 7. The little T is driveable and much heavier than it looks!

MAIN PIC: If one T bucket is good, then a whole line of them must be even better. This lot were participating in a recent cruise-in to the Autopia event at Autoplex Castlemaine and also visited various local hot rodders' workshops while in town. Rick Ling's turtledeck T leads the group, followed by Paul Turkentine's blue bucket.

BELOW: Wild flames, a healthy blown small block Chevy engine and wheelie bars out the back tell you this T bucket can get with the program. Owners Kevin and Lori Rendel fitted it with a 355 Chevy and Turbo 350 transmission.

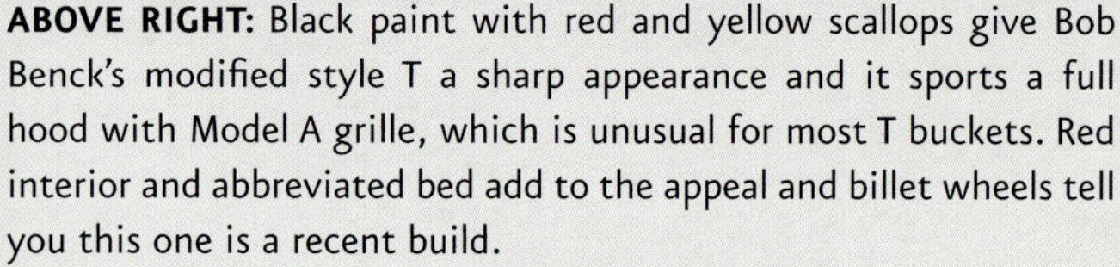

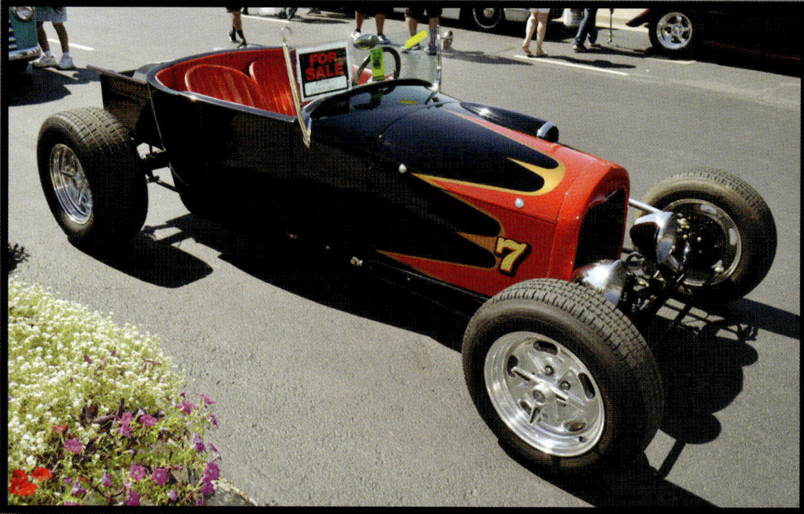

ABOVE RIGHT: Black paint with red and yellow scallops give Bob Benck's modified style T a sharp appearance and it sports a full hood with Model A grille, which is unusual for most T buckets. Red interior and abbreviated bed add to the appeal and billet wheels tell you this one is a recent build.

RIGHT: Time for another visit to the UK for a look at a home built green T bucket with small block Chevy engine and jaunty trunk at the back. Wheels are American five spokes and the T uses a cowl mounted steering system.

ABOVE: One more T from the Bonneville salt lake, this time a V windshield equipped version with round fuel tank, shortened Deuce grille and triple carb equipped small block Chevy engine.

ABOVE: Neil Cannan is the current custodian of this bucket with quite a history. Not a T but a later Model A, this one saw early drag racing on Victoria's Riverside drag strip and the Ballarat Airstrip. It's been deliberately kept in its "as-found" condition.

ABOVE: Bringing up the rear of this line of T buckets is Neville Field's "BLOWN T" that he has owned for so many years the velvet trim is starting to fade. This one is Ford powered.

RIGHT: One more for good measure, this time the stubby styled, low slung home built bucket of Rick Rufsvold that was photographed at the NSRA Nationals in Louisville, KY. A twin four equipped 265 Chevy with T10 four speed transmission provides the motivation. Looks like a fun drive!

NSRA NATS

Trends and Highlights from the past 35 years

Words: Larry O'Toole, Photos: Graffiti Archives

Looking back on the NSRA Street Rod Nationals over a long period of time gives readers the chance to reflect on how things have changed. Gathered together in this article from our archive files is a collection of representative photos of the trends and highlights over the years that we have attended the event. My first trip was to Oklahoma City in 1986 and, apart from 1987 when I went to the USA but didn't get to the Nationals, have attended every year until 2019. We all know how COVID-19 interrupted things in 2020, so even though the NSRA Nationals were held in 2020, in a somewhat smaller form, we were unable to attend due to international flight restrictions.

Since 2005 my son Allister has been a regular visitor to the NSRA Nationals as well. Between us we have taken countless thousands of photos that are all preserved in our archives, so there was plenty to select from for this review style article. Hope you enjoy this retrospective look at over 35 years of Nationals coverages.

ABOVE: Paint styles have typically changed quite a bit over the years. This photo is from 1991 when solid pastels were very trendy, but candy apple red never goes out of style. Bill Bowman owned the radically chopped 1937 Ford Tudor with smoothed-up, all peach painted body in the foreground.

ABOVE: This overall view of the thousands of street rods on the fairgrounds was taken from the chair lift at the 1990 event held in Columbus, Ohio. Something that is immediately noticeable about this scene is the number of non-Ford based street rods, but that's fairly typical of events in the American mid-west.

RIGHT: Track nosed T roadsters seem to wax and wane in popularity, but there is no doubt a well executed project like this one owned by Roger Ward from Ottawa, KS still turns heads. Photo is from Oklahoma City in 1986.

BELOW: Bumperless, monotone Buick two door retains minimal original stainless trim and features painted running boards. Another one from 1986.

RIGHT: Staying with 1986 we have another monochrome style rod, this time a smoothed up, chopped and bumperless '33 Ford sedan delivery.

BELOW: Egon Necelis stunned the Nationals crowd when he turned up in his wildly chopped and sectioned '40 La Salle sedan at Oklahoma City in 1986. Tunnelled headlights in moulded fenders and grille, plus louvered alligator style hood, late model mirrors, nerf bars and painted running boards demand a second look.

RIGHT: Flames never go out of style so this '40 Ford Tudor would still fit in today, perhaps sitting a little lower and with a change of wheel style.

BELOW: Classic styles here on a tidy wire wheeled '31 Model A Ford Victoria, the first year for this body style in the Model A range. The roadster behind is a '30 Model A with chrome wires, stock bumpers and cowl lights. This photo was taken in 1986 but could have been yesterday.

NSRA NATS 1986

ABOVE LEFT: Early Willys coupes like this maroon example were somewhat of a rarity at the Nationals, so it stood out when our photographer was passing by.

ABOVE: Graphics along the side of rods really started to kick off about this period (1986) and got more elaborate as the years passed, until they suddenly started to disappear again in the late nineties.

LEFT: During this same mid-eighties period we saw the emergence of really wild, blown big engines like the Chrysler Hemi in this '32 Ford three window coupe.

BELOW: We never have seen enough '26-'27 T Ford tourers given the street rod treatment and this one, photographed at Oklahoma City in 1986, shows they can fit right into any period style.

ABOVE: Classy fat fendered street rods like this '35 Ford Tudor would look right at home today. Update the wheels and it could be a current build rather than its 1986 heritage.

BELOW: Bright paint schemes stood out at Oklahoma City in 1986 and this trio of fat fendered Fords were typical. Left to right we have Jim Linton's green '35 Ford, Rick Love's flamed '39 Ford coupe and an unidentified bright red '40 Ford Standard coupe.

ABOVE: The owner of this one wanted his real steel '34 Ford roadster to stand apart from the growing number of reproduction versions, so he said so on the license plate.

BELOW: No doubt this one is real too! Chrome wires and stock body appointments make this burgundy '34 Ford tourer a classy piece and a rare sight at the NSRA Nationals in any period.

BOTTOM: There's always someone turning up in something to entertain the crowd in a different way. The "Rocket" is an old fairgrounds ride converted to street rod duty.

ABOVE: Yes, the owner was tall but his radically chopped, sectioned and full customised Mercury had the fans gob-smacked in the 1980s.

BELOW: Oh, I just thought I would bring my old '34 Ford roadster along to the Nationals! Next stop is the tractor pull!

ABOVE: I recall remarking at the time that one day someone would make a fortune out of supplying replacement fenderwells for early cars when the pro-street fad ended. It ended about 1995. This is Andy Wold's '32 Ford five window coupe from 1986.
BELOW: Good wheel to fender fit, smooth bodywork and bright red paint. It all adds up to state of the art street rod for any period.

ABOVE: Commercial rear bumpers on non-commercial body styles began to appear in the mid-'80s and remain popular today. This one is on Frantic Fred's '35 Ford flat back Tudor.
BELOW A different approach to the pro-street look was provided by this one in 1986 with hand made "Model A" that used dirt tracker tyres and competition style roll bar.

LEFT: Hiboy tourers aren't a new trend, this orange one with beige interior trim, is based on a '32 Ford and rolls on five spoke American Racing wheels that are back in vogue now and even reproduced in billet form. It was at the 1986 NSRA Nationals.
BELOW LEFT: Only the wheels give away the era of this Deuce hiboy roadster with Chevy emblem taillights and license plate frame. Okay, maybe the square headlights say 1986 too.

BELOW: By 1991 the graphics had become a little more refined but also more elaborate like the dual colour scallops on Dave Addison's Model A sedan delivery with suicide doors and chopped top.

LEFT: It looks like a cross continent racer from the thirties, but this '33 Ford roadster is from the 1989 NSRA Nationals. Bill and Sharon Davis drove it from from Oatonville, MI. The roadster features red interior trim, 7-ball shifter knob and small block Chevy engine.

BELOW: Not many Nashes get turned into street rods, but Fred Schutt from Colstup Montana bucked the trend with his lime green, small block Mopar powered version in 1989. Is that a hint of billet wheel peeking out from under the front fender?

BELOW LEFT: Dennis Kyle travelled all the way from southern California to St Paul, Minnesota in his Deuce hiboy for the NSRA Nationals in 1989. Dennis still owns the timeless hiboy and it still looks exactly the same.

BELOW: Pink scallops over blue paint and matching blue roof indicate a 1989 timeline for this hiboy '34 Ford roadster.

RIGHT: Cram a big block Chevy engine into a diminutive '48 Anglia Tudor in 1989 and people were bound to take notice. This was also about the time the "Chevy – Heartbeat of America" slogan appeared in advertising and spread to the enthusiast market. David Watkins owned this little terror.

BELOW: The American mid-west has always been an area where non-Ford based street rods proliferate. This example is a rare 1934 Pontiac straight eight cabriolet that's been restored and improved as a street rod by owner Ron Evans in 1989.

BELOW RIGHT: Boyce Asquith's wild Deuce hiboy roadster was a racer in street clothing that had a presence all of its own. Unfortunately it was wrecked in a racing accident that ended Boyce's life.

ABOVE: Nobody said you can't have a four wheel drive Model T Ford, so Gary Erikson took his to St Paul in 1989, all-terrain tyres and all!
RIGHT: Triple tone '47 Chevy sedan delivery was a high class street rod in 1988 with its smooth front roll pan, painted grille and dechromed bodywork. Owner was Tom Wilkinson from Sylvania, Ohio.

ABOVE: Two tone '37 Ford Tudor was a PPG Paint award winner at the 1989 NSRA Nats in St Paul. Owner Gary and Connie Stanifer from Whiteland, Indiana stripped all of the chrome and painted everything, including the bumpers.

ABOVE: In a similar manner Ted Zgryzemski's (Riverview, Michigan) chopped '37 Ford convertible was a PPG paint award winner at the same 1989 Nationals. Pale pastel peach was a popular choice at the time.

ABOVE: But red hot rods never go away, so this bunch of Willys coupes includes its fair share, along with a grey version and an orange one. For several years Willys owners had their own national gathering within the NSRA Nationals. This was 1989.

RIGHT: Tidy '35 Chevy two door sedan with filled, ribbed roof was right on the current trend when it appeared at the NSRA Nationals in 1991. It was small block Chevy powered and owned by Wallace Scales of Garland TX. The aqua '33 Ford three window coupe next in line was also small block Chevy powered and belonged to Ron and Kathie Kurth while Chuck and Linda Barker from Simi Valley CA owned the yellow '35 Ford Tudor with chromed and painted wire wheels.

LEFT: A chopped and sectioned '40 Ford Standard coupe with no polished trim anywhere on the customised body looks slick in candy apple red paint right down to the running boards. Note the frenched headlights, painted grille and swoopy lines of the sectioned hood. Chrome plated wheels with gold plated spinners add the only polished highlights that obviously caught the young onlookers attention. Wonder if he has his own hot rod now?

ABOVE: At the height of the pro-street era, the huge wheel tubs almost entirely fill the trunk of Tom Doepke's '40 Willys coupe at the 1993 NSRA Nationals. Brodix equipped blown big block Chevy running gear matched the look and it also featured a grey interior and Center Line Wheels.

ABOVE: Hemi engine in a T Tudor was a rare sight back in 1991. Jenny Eatherman's has lengthened wheelbase to allow enough room for the big donk to fit in the otherwise small engine bay. Next in line is a peach 1934 Chevy cabriolet owned by Henry Esposito while the magenta pink chopped '40 Ford sedan belonged to Chuck and Judy Irons.
BELOW RIGHT: Sweet Model A roadster pickup retains most of its original appointments but with a dropped headlight bar and radical lowering giving it the perfect stance.

BELOW: Nostalgia never goes out of style. This Deuce roadster was entered by George Poteet and featured four banger power with Miller head, twin 97s and 1935 Ford wire wheels back in 1990. George has gone on to achieve a few other things in hot rodding and dry lakes racing since then.
BELOW RIGHT: Larry and Sherry Stewart's severely chopped 1941 Chevy coupe had painted side trim and was stripped of all stainless trim. Engine was a tunnel ram equipped Chevy.

ABOVE: Bud Wagner brought his two tone scalloped pink '33 Ford three window coupe from Lake County, OH in 1990. It had matching colours interior trim.
BELOW: Pete Aardema's all white '33 Ford coupe sported a small block Chevy engine that was east-west mounted in the trunk!. Lots of trick engineering throughout this car that Pete still owns today. This photo was taken in 1991.

ABOVE: Orange and super rare '32 Ford B400 stood out in 1991. Greg Morris of Hugoton, KS was the lucky owner of the small block Chevy powered beauty with beige interior and tilt steering column.
BELOW: Desirable '33 Dodge pickup from the 1990 Nationals was finished in bright red paint with polished five spoke wheels and beige vinyl covered tonneau.

ABOVE: Anglia derivatives have always been popular in American hot rodding as evidenced by this pair. The '48 delivery van has a neat fold-back sun roof, 305 Chevy engine with Powerglide transmission, independent front suspension and 12 bolt Chevy rear end. It was owned by Arhie McDiarmid, while the black and chopped two door was fitted with a healthy small block Chevy engine and featured a tube chassis. Interior trim was yellow and blue.

ABOVE: Lots of custom touches on this '38 Chevy two door sedan including suicide doors and side opening trunk. By 1991 the billet wheel movement was under way, so this big block Chevy powered street rod was right up there with the current all-painted/ no polished trim trends of the time for owners Mike and Cathie Shelton.

ABOVE RIGHT: Also from 1991 was this grape coloured '38 Ford Standard coupe that featured Weld Wheels, V-butted windshield glass and fancy, graphic pinstriping.

RIGHT: Bright orange Deuce hiboy roadster had instant appeal to me thanks to the namesake license plate. Flush fitting fuel filler door and smooth, roll panned body at the rear were in vogue in 1991 and added to the appeal of Larry's hiboy.

ABOVE: Colorful line up of rods is at the 1991 Nationals and shows an almost continuous line of '32 Ford roadsters – just one yellow '33 model sneaking in as well. The black Deuce with flames looks like a clone of Tom McMullen's famous '32 Ford roadster with full fenders added.

ABOVE: 1941 Ford Woody owned by Dale Boesch. Amongst its many features were fully contoured leather interior, injected 351 Cleveland engine and polished American five spoke wheels. It was the Aussies' pick at the 1991 Nats.
ABOVE LEFT: Ken Fenical (Posies) set some radical new trends in his time and the 1990 Nationals example was no exception. Wildly restyled, the 1932 Ford three window coupe featured matching oval shaped headlights, mirrors and taillights along with a host of other individual touches.
LEFT: All paint finished '40 Ford Standard convertible even had painted running boards and headlight rims, along with a couple of inches out of the windscreen frame.

MAIN PIC: There were some trick ideas incorporated in this '35 Ford, in particular note how the bottom of the grille has been modified for extra clearance. Owner was David Roberts of Brookfield Colorado, engine was small block Chevy and the Tudor also featured a grey interior and Budnick wheels. No details on the blue '32 Ford three window coupe, but the lilac coupe in the background was Ben Watson's '33 Ford.

ABOVE: Local rodder Roy Poindexter debuted his wild 1948 Ford roadster pickup at the 1991 Nats (Oklahoma City) that features pastel green paint, tilt and tubbed bed and tunnel ram equipped big block Chev engine.

LEFT: Awesome Pro-street Styled '40 Ford Standard Tudor was a real attention grabber at the 1990 NSRA Nats in Columbus, OH. Owner Alfred Adams outfitted the '40 with a blown big block Chevy.

ABOVE: Big Buicks from the late fifties and early sixties almost look like full customs even in stock form. This pair made it even more pronounced by parking side by side at the Sunday morning show in downtown Cowes.

The KOA Kustom Nationals at Phillip Island was held a week later than usual to stay clear of the big tourist rush on the island over the New Year holiday period. Since the event was moved from the Phillip Island race circuit a couple of years ago, it is now held from the middle of the day on Saturday through to 8:oopm in the evening at San Remo foreshore and on Sunday it moves to the jetty area at Cowes. The Saturday show at San Remo was huge, filling the entire allocated space with a fantastic collection of customs and special cars, made up mostly of street rods and classics. The organisers try to assemble the show and shine with all of the top full Kustoms and street rods in the main exhibit area and this worked very well on this occasion,

RIGHT: Side shot of this Custom '54 Chevy two door sedan reveals its low, slightly tail dragger stance and straight bodywork.

ABOVE: Big, black and all Cadillac seems an appropriate description for this outstanding '60 Coupe De Ville with graphic rooftop paint.

the entire "select" area being filled with really high quality cars. Sunday was much the same in downtown Cowes but the numbers had reduced a bit due to some participants electing to attend on one day only.

This year the Kustom Nats was a drive-up-and-pay-at-the-gate affair, so there was no pre-entry to pay, or entry form information gathered. That made our job a little harder when trying to identify vehicle owners in this coverage, so if your name is missing off the photo of your car in this article, that's the reason.

The Kustom Nats is a must-do event on the Southern Australian car scene calendar and that looks likely to continue.

LEFT: Superbly turned out '54 Mercury Victoria with well executed scallops over pearl bronze and white paintwork demands attention from passers by.

BELOW: Full custom Ford coupe is actually built over a Holden floor pan and running gear buy owner Brenton Creasy. Lakes pipes and Caddy wheel covers that don't turn with the wheels are other notable features.

BELOW: Banger engine with overhead valve conversion in a stock bodied Deuce coupe came from a private collection in the USA, but is now owned by Greg Klun.

BELOW: Scalloped paintwork over green and low riding stance make this XP Falcon station wagon a stand out entry.

RIGHT: Smooth looking custom XP Falcon ute has a hard tonneau over the cargo area and louvred sunshade in the rear window.

ABOVE: That's a later model Holden V8 swapped into the engine bay of this FX Holden mild custom. Maroon paint and Cragar S/S wheels suit it down to the ground.

ABOVE: It was too late model to be an official entrant, but Craig Harris'. FC/Commodore hybrid custom certainly turned heads at San Remo on the Friday evening. There's no doubt it's a well executed custom.

LEFT: HD-HR era Holdens have a strong following and now wonder when they are given the smooth, semi-custom treatment exemplified by this blue example. Matching painted spoke billet wheels set this HD off even more.

BELOW: A '55 Chevy Sports Coupe in bare metal is alway going to attract more than its fair share of attention. This one also has tinted glass and polished Centre Line wheels.

LEFT: The radical treatment given to this red Chevy pickup means it attracts lots of attention from the spectators.
BELOW: Low rider '48 Chevy two door sedan features a dechromed body with satin green paintwork, frenched headlights and paint detailed chrome rims.

ABOVE: Any Cadillac has a presence just by its sheer size but none more so than this pale beige '55 Coupe De Ville.

ABOVE: Style in abundance oozes from Dave Werkmuller's bright red '57 Ford two door sedan. The Y block engine in the engine bay shot at top right attracts the attention of some patrons.

ABOVE: Old Holdens are making a comeback and they often have a surprise in the engine bay like the one on the right that has a Toyota V8 engine fitted. The green one has a more traditional twin carb equipped grey motor.

LEFT: Down from Queensland was Dale Haberfield and Paul McMullin in these race inspired '32 Ford hiboy roadsters. Both are flathead V8 powered with finned heads and the black one is topped with a blower.

BELOW: Jamie Camilleri's brilliant gold Deuce five window coupe is stand out street rod that turns heads every time it show up. In the engine bay is a six carb equipped Y block Ford engine and the interior trim is pure white rolled and pleated vinyl. That's Darren Newton's from Spades Rod & Custom Club metallic blue F100 pickup next door.

LEFT: A Chevy pickup with a well executed patina finish sits low to the ground and looks like a fun ride. This one belongs to Joe Vanuttini.

ABOVE: Typical of the variety of vehicle that turn up for the KOA Nats Beach Party is this pair. The rare Chevy wagon belongs to Robert Wakartschuk, while Michelle Forward owns the Model A Ford street rod roadster.

LEFT: VW Kombis turn up to the KOA event every year with beauties like these prominent in the show area.

RIGHT: Some of young pinstriper, Lincoln Camilleri's handiwork on display.

ABOVE: Classy is the only way to describe Blacktop Cruisers Rod & Custom Club founding member Mark Magill's '49 Olds sedanette that rolls on chrome wheels with whitewall tyres.

RIGHT: Innocent looking HG Holden panel van was filled with late model Commodore V8 running gear, including the independent rear end and dash.

BELOW: A shady parking spot is appreciated by Dean's mild custom '52 Mercury hardtop and the bright blue hiboy '33 Ford coupe of Clint Chedwiggen, both from the Spades.

ABOVE: Doug Smith's split window '34 Ford hiboy coupe shares parking space with Dave Monaghan's 409 powered '32 three window coupe.

ABOVE: You're never too young to get involved in the Kustom scene as evidenced by this picture of young Lincoln Camilleri plying his talents as an accomplished pinstriper on the rear of a Customline.

LEFT: Dieter Edelmaier often brings his green '34 Ford hiboy roadster to the KOA Natioonals. Chrome wheels with whitewalls and tan interior are just a couple of the features of this Ford powered roadster.

BELOW: It's a regular at KOA events but you never tire of seeing Paul Vanzella's custom two tone pink and chopped '60 Dodge Pioneer. It glides along the street like the perfect piece of artwork that it represents. Chrome wire spoke wheels and whitewalls don't hurt the image either.

BELOW & RIGHT: Really nice HK Holden ute has just enough mild custom touches to set it apart and the quality of finish is second to none.

ABOVE RIGHT: Bright orange paint and a prominent scoop makes this Cortina stand out from mundane stock versions. There's a roll cage inside indicating that this one might see some competition use too.

www.graffitipub.com.au

ABOVE: Steve Brown likes to sit and sketch the custom car scene as it evolves around him. Steve's artwork was featured in HRI #7.
LEFT: A wild custom grille insert is just right on Rob Hannam's '58 Chevy.
BELOW LEFT: Dietmar Munnecke's flathead powered Model A coupe.
BELOW: Pristine '34 Ford Victoria is a rare car in Australia and this one retains all of its original Ford accessories.

ABOVE: John Katsanis is no longer with us but his legacy lives on and his flathead powerd Deuce hiboy roadster still takes pride of place at the Kustom Nationals Beach Party.
RIGHT: Red oxide suits the workmanlike stature of Luke Katsanis' '41 Ford pickup that rolls on steel wheels with caps and trim rings.

ABOVE: What's not to like about a two tone '55 Pontiac coupe with subtle scallops off the fenderwell, full wheel caps and whitewall tyres.

ABOVE: Who says a New York Chequer Cab can't be a custom? Being parked beside a mean '49 Dodge pickup gives you an idea of the cab's size.

ABOVE: A nice top chop and flawless red paint make Paul Naughton's '48 Ford convertible stand apart. Right behind it is Paul 's other car, a beautiful gold and black '50 Ford custom with chopped top and louvered hood amongst its many other modifications.

ABOVE LEFT: Ponder a little while on this immaculate Porsche in perfect glossy black with red interior.
LEFT: This early fifties Bedford might look like it came straight from the barn on the farm but underneath it was fully rebuilt in typical street rod fashion.

ABOVE: Joe Amato's trick 1951 Chevy Deluxe coupe sports a chopped top, mile deep candy paintwork and the grille from a 1949 Cadillac. Opposite is a superb gold and bronze '54 Chevy with smoothed hood and many extra teeth in the grille and fresh Victorian rego plates.